Visual Literacy

How to Read and Use Information in Graphic Form

Marcia Weaver

LearningExpress

NEW YORK

Library of Congress Cataloging-in-Publication Data

Weaver, Marcia.
   Visual literacy / by Marcia Weaver.
      p.   cm.
   ISBN 1–57685–223–7
   1. Communication—Audio-visual aids.   I. Title.
P93.5.W43   1999
302.23—dc21   99-28919
                                                        CIP

Printed in the United States of America
9 8 7 6 5 4 3 2 1
First Edition

For Further Information
For information on LearningExpress, other LearningExpress products, or bulk sales, please write to us at:

> LearningExpress®
> 900 Broadway
> Suite 604
> New York, NY 10003

Visit LearningExpress on the World Wide Web at www.LearnX.com.

Contents

Introduction   v

Pretest   1

Chapter 1   The Picture Tells the Story: Graphic Formats   19

Chapter 2   The Key Is the Key: How to Use Titles, Legends, and Measurements to Read Graphics   35

Chapter 3   Beyond Road Maps: Types, Use, and Interpretation of Map Graphics   43

Chapter 4   Keeping Track of Information: Checksheets, Logs, and Tables   53

Chapter 5   Crunching Numbers: Spreadsheets   65

Chapter 6   Information in a Block: Bar Graphs and Column Graphs   73

Chapter 7   Information in a Line: Line Graphs   83

Chapter 8   Shape Things Up with Histograms   93

Chapter 9   The 80/20 Rule: Pareto Charts and Their Use in Problem Solving   103

Chapter 10   Stay within the Lines: Run Charts and Control Charts   111

Chapter 11   It Matters How You Slice It: Pie Charts   119

Chapter 12   X Marks the Spot: Point Graphs and Scattergrams   129

Chapter 13   Problem Solving with Fishbone Diagrams   139

Chapter 14   Go with the Flow: Flowcharts   147

Chapter 15   Keep It Moving: Gantt and PERT Charts   155

Chapter 16   Who's Who and What's What: Tree Diagrams and Organization Charts   163

Chapter 17   Blueprints 101: Blueprints and Drawings   173

Chapter 18   Schematics 101: Electronic Diagrams and Symbols   181

Chapter 19   What You See Is What You Get: Spatial/Visual Intelligence   191

Answer Key   205

Posttest   225

Bibliography   245

About the Author

Marcia Weaver is a training and development consultant in Glendale, California. She designs and implements basic work skill training programs, including visual literacy and document literacy skills, for employees in both the manufacturing and service sectors. She holds a master of science degree from the University of San Francisco and membership in the American Society for Quality.

Introduction

Three separate occurrences have increased the need for visual literacy in today's world. These are globalization, increased computer usage, and employee involvement in total quality improvement.

First, globalization—doing business with the rest of the world—requires multicultural work teams that can understand concepts and problem solve in a common language. The most common language of all is graphic language, or symbols. Think of finding your way in a foreign airport. It's not the written language that is most helpful—it is the international symbols that help you find the bathrooms, the coffee shop, the bus, and many other necessities.

Visual displays of information are becoming more important every day in the world of work and daily living. Symbols communicate ideas across cultures more quickly and accurately than verbal language. As Tim W. Ferguson says in his December 14, 1998 article "Drawing Room" in *Forbes* magazine, "We are becoming a more visual and less textual people… what was verbal is becoming visual."

Second, computers are capable of digesting huge amounts of information and quickly producing the results in graphic form, thereby making the results easier to understand. Possible outcomes can be grasped at a glance without sorting through massive amounts of data. AS Edward R. Tufte in *Visual Display of Quantitative Information* says, "Data graphics are universal and not tied to any language."

It is this quick understanding of important concepts that drives the use of more and more graphic displays of information in business. Managers need to communicate ideas at a glance, and visual displays accomplish this where verbal presentations alone are often not enough.

Third, employee involvement in the "grand scheme" of a business has put statistical graphs in the view of almost every employee. Flowcharts and statistics have become a part of everyday work life because they communicate so much about product quality without using a lot of words. One look and you know whether your product quality is improving or deteriorating. You can check the "scoreboard" as often as you like to see how you're doing.

Where Will You Find Visual Displays of Data?

You will find visual displays everywhere, including the following:

- in newspapers to present information; i.e. stocks, weather, sports, and population distribution
- in magazines—to support articles on automobiles, sports, financial, computers, business, science, and health
- on television—weather, sports (remember the Olympics?), business information, and politics (remember Ross Perot and his charts in the 1992 political campaign?)
- in text books
- in travel guides
- as diagrams for assembling furniture or toys
- in technical manuals
- in every part of any business involved in quality improvement efforts
- on signs in national parks and tourist facilities
- on computer screens and in software programs
- on the walls in your boss' office!

Since graphic displays of data are just about everywhere, you will increase your ability to function in the business world when you become familiar with graphics.

Why You Need to Become Visually Literate

Although we know we need to read graphics, many of us did not learn much about it in school. Business leaders complain that new employees lack this skill. This lack of skill is probably highlighted by the increased necessity to read graphics and interpret them in the workplace. According to a National Association of Manufacturers (NAM) survey issued November 14, 1997:

- 48% said that too many of their workers lack the ability to read and interpret drawings, diagrams, and flow charts

- 73% said that they either cannot improve productivity or upgrade technology due to skill deficiencies

This information indicates that you will be more marketable as a worker when you increase your ability to read graphic data displays.

This book will show you how to read a graphic data display quickly and accurately. It will give you a practical approach to unlocking the secrets of data display and using it for analyzing and solving problems. You will also be able to create some graphic displays of your own and you will be better prepared for today's workplace.

After you have finished studying the 19 lessons in this book, you will have mastered the seven necessary steps to reading a graphic. These seven steps are outlined in the box to the right.

The Seven Steps to Reading a Graphic

1. **Identify the format**—What do you think of when you see a specific graphic format?
2. **Study the title**—What is the purpose or main idea behind the graphic?
3. **Interpret the text and labels**—What are the components of the chart?
4. **Analyze the legends**—Are the components identified by special symbols, patterns, or colors? What do abbreviations mean?
5. **Determine the measurement and the components**—What is being measured, how often, and by what measurement?
6. **Write two questions about the graphic**—What are two things you want to know as you look at the display? Find the answers.
7. **Review the total graphic**—Does your analysis fit with your first impression of the graphic?

Pretest

Before you start your quest to become visually literate, you may want to get an idea of how much you already know and how much you need to learn. If that's the case, take the pretest in this chapter.

The pretest contains 35 multiple-choice questions that offer a sampling of topics covered in the book. You'll get to try your hand at reading information from many of the most common types of charts and graphs, as well as test your current knowledge of other visual forms such as maps, schedules, and scattergrams. Some of these forms are more common than others and will look familiar; others may be new to you.

So use this pretest just to get a general idea of how much of what's in this book you already know. If you get a high score on this pretest, you may be able to spend less time with this book than you originally planned. If you get a low score, you may find that you will need more than 20 minutes a day to get through each chapter and learn all of the words.

Take as much time as you need to do this short test. Simply circle the answer numbers in this book. If the book doesn't belong to you, write the numbers 1–35 on a piece of paper and record your answers there. When you finish, check your answers against the answer key at the end of this chapter. Each answer tells you which chapter of this book teaches you about the graphics in that question.

Use the map on the next page to answer questions 1–3.

1. Leon Woolf has a one hour break from his job at Livingston Mall and plans to drive to his grandmother's house at the southwest corner of Canyon Drive and Linda Lane for lunch. Which of the following is the most direct legal route?
   a. Turn north on Amhoy Road, then east on Linda Lane, then north on Canyon Drive.
   b. Turn east on McMahon Street, then north on El Camino, then west on Linda Lane, then north on Orinda Road, then east on Barcelona Blvd. to Canyon Drive.
   c. Turn north on Amhoy Road, then east on Barcelona Blvd., then south on Canyon Drive.

2. After getting off work at the Municipal Parking Lot, Jamal Ortiz needs to go to a friend's house at the northeast corner of Barcelona Blvd. and James Avenue. Which is the most direct legal route for him to drive?
   a. North on Orinda Road, west on Linda Lane, then north on James Avenue.
   b. West on McMahon Street, north on Livingston Avenue, then east on Barcelona to James Avenue.
   c. North on Amhoy Road, then west on Barcelona Blvd. to James Avenue.

3. Ricky Ricardo is driving west on Bortz Road. He makes a right turn onto James Avenue, then a left onto Linda Lane, then a right again onto Livingston, and then another right onto Barcelona Blvd. What direction is he facing?
   a. east   b. south   c. west   d. north

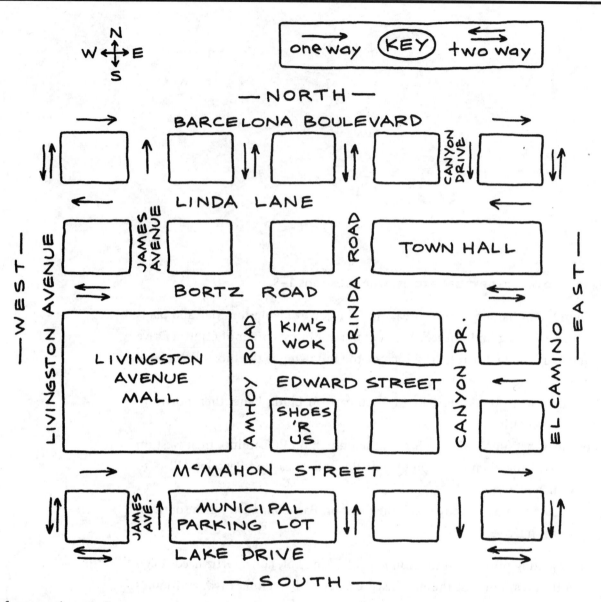

Map for questions 1–3

Blue route bus schedule

	Depot	Washington St.
Bus 1	6:00	6:53
Bus 2	6:30	7:23
Bus 3	7:00	7:53
Bus 4	7:20	8:03
Bus 5	7:40	8:33

Schedule for question 4

Use the schedule to answer question 4.

4. What time is Bus 2 scheduled to arrive at Washington St.?

   a. 6:53   b. 7:23   c. 7:53

Pet grooming for week of June 7-12

Animal	Bathe	Clean Teeth	Clip Nails
Dogs	✓✓✓	✓✓	✓✓
Cats	✓✓✓	✓✓✓	✓✓✓
Birds	✓✓		✓
Iguanas	✓✓✓	✓✓	✓✓✓

Checksheet for question 5

Use the checksheet to answer question 5.

5. Which was the grooming activity most often requested for iguanas?

   a. bathing   b. teeth-cleaning   c. nail-clipping

Bob & Nadine's Wedding Check Register

Date	Check #	Item	Deposit	Withdrawal	Balance
1-June		Bob's parents	2,000		2,000
1-June		Nadine's grandma	1,000		3,000
4-June	700	Nadine's dress		400.98	2,599.02
5-June	701	Bob's tux rental		150.76	2,448.26
5-June	702	Caterer (Bob's cousin Larry)		100.00	2,348.26
6-June	703	Flowers R Us		600.00	1,748.26
7-June		Check 702 stop payment fee		5.00	1,743.26
9-June	704	Caterer (Good Eats Bar & Grill)		500.00	1,243.26
11-June	705	Announcements		151.76	1,091.50
11-June		Correction: Check 702 stopped	100		1,191.50
12-June	706	Bail for Larry		250.00	941.50
15-June	707	Minister fee		25.00	916.50
16-June		Gift from Bob's Uncle Fred	100		1,016.50
16-June	708	Used car for honeymoon trip		800	216.50
17-June	709	Bridal Suite, Marina Motel		180	36.50
21-June	710	Marina Motel coffee shop wedding breakfast		35.37	1.13

Spreadsheet for questions 6 and 7

Use the spreadsheet to answer questions 6 and 7.

6. Bob and Nadine have opened a special checking account to handle their wedding expenditures. Which check was written for an expenditure NOT directly related to their nuptials?

_____

7. What was the balance in Bob and Nadine's account just before the deposit of the gift from Uncle Fred?
   a. $916.50   b. $1,016.50   c. $836.50

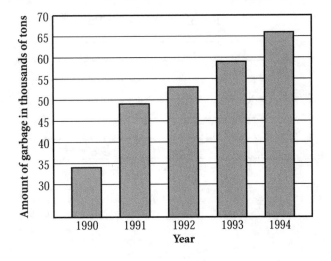

Bar graph for questions 8 and 9

Use the bar graph to answer questions 8 and 9.

8. How many more thousands of tons of garbage were generated in 1994 than in 1993?

   a. about 66,000   b. about 59,000   c. about 7,000

9. The most logical reason for creating this bar graph would be to support

   a. a request for funds to hire additional Sanitation Department personnel in 1995

   b. consolidation of routes as a Sanitation Department cost-cutting effort in 1995

   c. a request for funds for safer Sanitation Department toxic waste disposal in 1995

Use the line graph on the next page to answer questions 10 and 11.

10. How much rainfall was there in March 1996?

   a. 0″   b. 2″   c. 4″

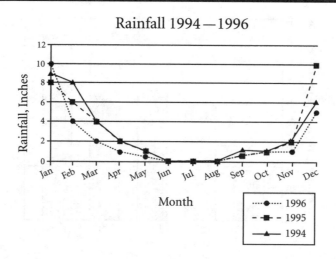

Line graph for questions 10 and 11

11. What was the difference in rainfall between December 1994 and December 1996?

a. In 1994, about 1″ more rain fell than in 1996.

b. In 1994, about 1/2″ less rain fell than in 1996.

c. In 1994, about 2″ more rain fell than in 1996.

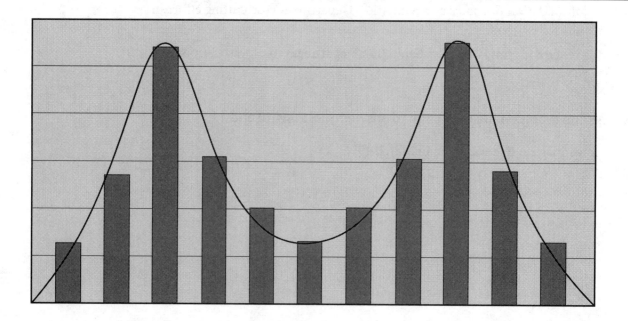

Graphic for questions 12 and 13

Use the graphic on the previous page to answer questions 12 and 13.

12. The histogram shown is a good example of a
    a. bell curve   b. a skewed curve   c. a bi-modal curve

13. Which of the following does this curve likely indicate?
    a. The data was produced by more than one process.
    b. There are two possible interpretations of the data.
    c. The data likely contains error.

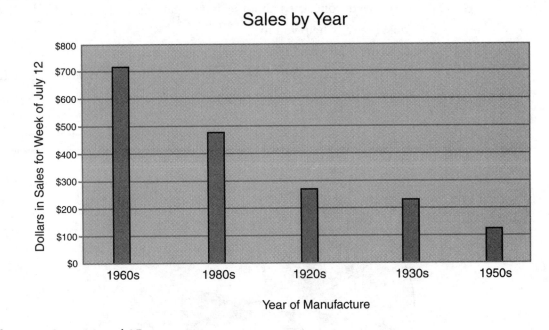

Chart for questions 14 and 15

Use the chart to answer questions 14 and 15.

14. Larelda owns a small antique clothing store in which the stock is arranged by year of manufacture. She is planning to rearrange the stock, moving the best-selling items toward the front and those that do not sell so well toward the back. According to the chart, how will the items be ordered, front to back?

    _____

    Explain your answer.

    _____

15. Clothing from the 1950s brought in how many dollars in sales over the five days?
    a. $0   b. $100   c. $120

16. Following are lines that might be found on a control chart.

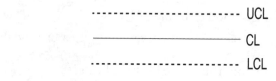

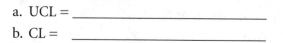

Identify those lines:

a. UCL = _____

b. CL = _____

c. LCL = _____

17. If you were concerned about losing or gaining weight, a control chart would most logically help you to

a. record your weight loss or weight gain over time

b. decide which weight-loss or weight-gain diet would be most beneficial

c. maintain your desirable weight

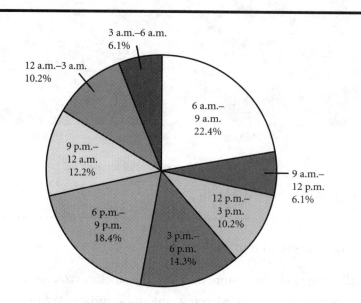

Pie chart for questions 18 and 19

Answer questions 18 and 19 on the basis of the pie chart, which shows the percentage of home fires in a certain neighborhood for various times of day.

18. According to the chart, a home fire has the greatest probability of starting at which of the following times?

a. 12:19 p.m.   b. 9:30 p.m.   c. 7:23 a.m.

19. This chart would most logically be used for the purpose of deciding
    a. the best content for future community fire safety classes
    b. which firehouse shift needs to recruit extra volunteer firefighters
    c. whether extra firefighting equipment is needed in this neighborhood

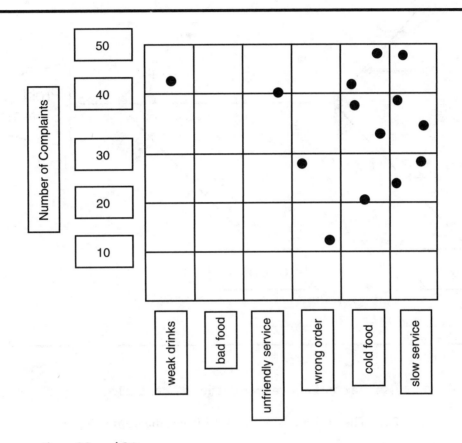

Scattergram for questions 20 and 21

Use the scattergram to answer questions 20 and 21.

20. Fannie's Foxhead Tavern has begun serving food as well as drinks, and has had a barrage of complaints. Fannie decides to do something about it and begins by making a point graph to study the problem. Based on the graph, which of her staff should she consider replacing?
    a. her waitstaff   b. her cook   c. her bartender

21. What is the usual purpose of a scattergram?
    a. to study the relationship of one variable to another
    b. to detect a trend
    c. to enumerate steps in a process

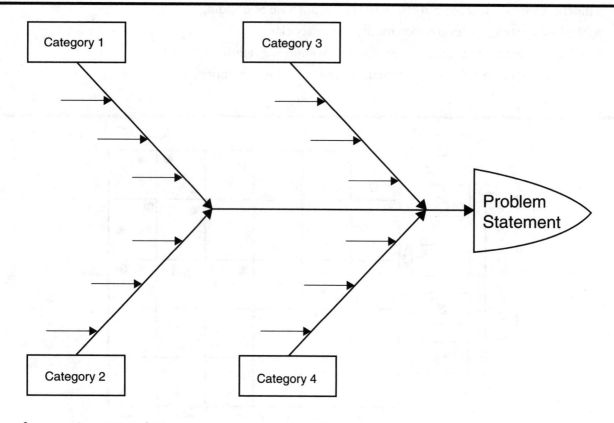

Chart for questions 22 and 23

Use the chart above for questions 22 and 23.

22. The diagram is called an Ishikawa diagram or a

_____

23. The diagram pictured is usually arrived at
   a. by a group in a brainstorming session
   b. by the head of the organization involved
   c. as the final step of a long project

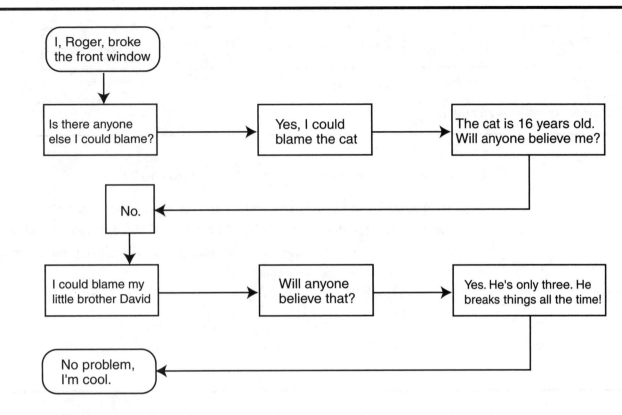

Flowchart for questions 24 and 25

___

Use the flowchart to answer questions 24 and 25.

24. What does the flowchart represent?
   a. a thinking-through process
   b. a compendium of facts
   c. a "to do" list

25. What do the ovals on the flowchart represent?
   a. decision points in a process
   b. the beginning or end of a process
   c. steps in a process

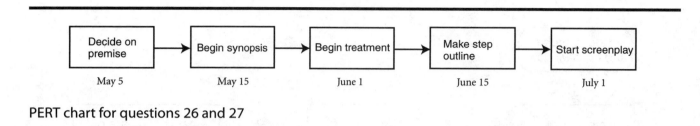

PERT chart for questions 26 and 27

Use the PERT chart above to answer questions 26 and 27.

26. Myra has decided to write a screenplay and has made a PERT chart outlining the steps and the deadlines she has set for herself. According to the chart, how much time will elapse between the time she makes the step outline and the time she begins the screenplay?
    a. half a month   b. 20 days   c. 1 month

27. As pictured here, the PERT chart is really a form of
    a. scattergram   b. fishbone chart   c. flowchart

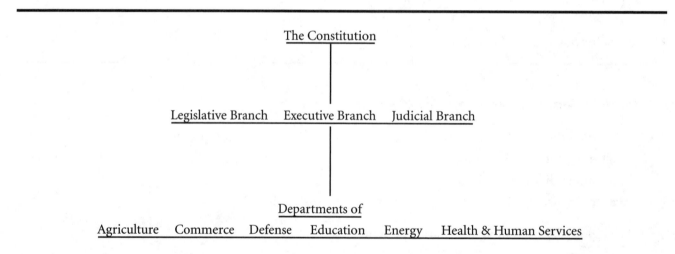

Tree diagram for questions 28 and 29

28. The graphic of the U.S. Federal Government is called a "divergent" tree diagram. It is called this because
    a. each branch represents an autonomous entity
    b. the origin of the branches is the most significant entry
    c. all branches fork from a single branch

29. This graphic is also an "organizational" diagram and one of its functions is to help us discern the organizational
    a. hierarchy   b. functions   c. services

30. A blueprint is created so that

    a. the designer can communicate uniform directions to the people who make the product

    b. the people who make the product can communicate uniform directions to the designer

    c. the designer can keep track of the steps he or she has to take along the way to the finished product

31. Which of the following are you likely to find on a blueprint?

    a. price   b. scale   c. section number

A

B

Electronics diagram for questions 32 and 33

---

32. What do symbols A and B in the graphic stand for?

    a. A = capacitor; B = amplifier

    b. A = transistor, n-p-n; B = connector

    c. A = terminal; B = ground, general

33. Where would you be most likely to find this symbol?

    a. on a schematic   b. on a component   c. on a rendering

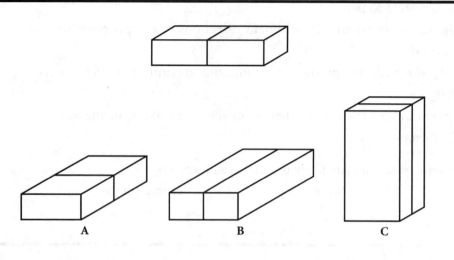

Graphic for questions 34 and 35

Use the graphic to answer questions 34 and 35.

34. Which of the three lettered figures could be the unlettered (top) figure, seen from a different angle?
a. C only   b. A and B   c. B and C   d. A only

35. Which of the following exercises would be most likely to improve your spatial/visual intelligence?
a. drawing from memory
b. memorizing a poem
c. doing algebra problems

Answers

1. **c.** This is the simplest, most direct way around the one-way streets and Town Hall.

2. **a.** The other routes require illegal maneuvers.

3. **a.** Right on James leaves Ricky heading north. Left on Linda is west; right on Livingston is north. Right on Barcelona, then, leave Ricky going east.

4. **b.** Read across from Bus 2 until you get to the Washington St. column.

5. **c.** There are more hatchmarks in the column headed "Clip Nails" than in the other columns.

6. Check #706 was written for Larry's bail.

7. **a.** You must look at the entry *above* Uncle Fred's check.

8. **c.** The difference between approximately 66,000 tons in 1994 and about 59,000 tons in 1993 is 7,000 tons.

9. **a.** The graph strongly suggests that the Sanitation Department will be required to handle much more garbage in 1995, which supports choice **a.** The other two choices are not closely related to an increase in the overall amount of garbage to be handled.

10. **b.** Look at the dotted line for 1996.

11. **a.** Look at the solid line and at the densely dotted lines for December.

12. **c.** Note the two high points on the curve—"twin peaks." The name of this kind of curve, which includes the prefix "bi" (two), indicates its shape.

13. **a.** The data might be from two manufacturers, say, or from two machines.

14. 1960s, 1980s, 1920s, 1930s, 1950s. The horizontal axis of the chart is read from left to right, best sales to worst sales.

15. **c.** The bar for 1950 is a little over the $100 line.

16. UCL = upper control limit; CL = center line (or average of all the averages); LCL = lower control limit.

17. **c.** The purpose of a control chart is to control a process, so the answer is **c.**

18. **c.** See the section for fires starting between 6:00 a.m. and 9:00 a.m.

19. **b.** The information on the pie chart pertains only to time of day and not to safety or types of equipment.

20. **a.** Most of the points on the graph have to do with waitstaff service.

21. **a.** Two variables might be, for example, monthly income and frequency of eating out. The scattergram would help answer the question: Exactly how does the first affect the second?

22. Fishbone diagram.

23. **a.** The fishbone diagram is usually used in the early stages of problem solving, when members of a team are coming up with tentative ideas.

24. **a.** By means of this flowchart, Roger is thinking through ways to keep out of trouble.
25. **b.** Ovals represent stopping or starting points in a process.
26. **a.** From June 15 to July 1 is about half a month.
27. **c.** The PERT chart, like the flowchart, describes steps in a process.
28. **c.** All branches fork or *diverge* from a single branch.
29. **a.** The graphic shows the Federal Government hierarchy.
30. **a.** The blueprint is a visual communication tool from designer to producer.
31. **b.** The scale tells you whether the drawing is bigger, smaller, or the same size at the real thing, and by how much.
32. **c.** A is a terminal, B is a ground.
33. **a.** These are common symbols found on an electronics schematic.
34. **d.** Figure A is the unlettered object, as seen from the end.
35. **a.** Drawing will help you picture an object in space. The other two choices are more likely to improve your linguistic intelligence or logical-mathematical intelligence.

Chapter 1

The Picture Tells the Story

Graphic Formats

This chapter introduces the main graphic display formats and describes their use. After completing the exercises on the following pages, you will be able to recognize these graphics anywhere you see them. This is the first step in understanding visual displays of information.

The Value of Graphic Display

When data is transformed into a graphic, the data must be summarized. The graphic shows the main points to be considered, or the results, and is much simpler to read. You don't have to sift through hundreds of unnecessary words in order to select what is important—the sifting is done for you. For this reason, you may be able to understand statistical data better if they are displayed in graphic form.

The person who creates the graph is like a translator who takes the verbal information and turns it into a picture. In this case, a picture is worth a thousand words: The main concepts that the data represent will stand out clearly in the graphic representation. You can take in the main idea of the data summary all at once. Then you can go back and look at the details and do your own investigation into the data if you still need more information.

If you learn more easily with pictures than with words and numbers, graphs will help you better understand the data. If you have to analyze results in a hurry, graphs will give you the summarized statistical data you need in a timely way.

Today, graphical display of numerical data is used as a tool for analyzing the data as well as displaying and presenting it. It is useful for analysis because it engages your whole brain and provides something for every type of learner. The data are there for you to analyze—but the visual display of the results does a lot of the work for you.

What the Pictures Tell You

A graph, chart, or other informational graphic usually presents the results of a data analysis or study. It displays the main points of the data so that you can understand the information immediately. The main purpose, goal, or idea for the data presentation should determine the format of the graphic.

Some of the most common graphic formats are:

- maps
- tables
- spreadsheets
- pie charts
- bar graphs or column graphs
- line graphs
- fishbone diagrams
- flowcharts
- tree diagrams
- organization charts
- Gantt charts

Each of these formats, without specific data, communicates the main idea of the graphic and the summary of information.

Overview of Graphic Formats

Maps

A good example of a graphic format that communicates an idea is a map. You probably see maps every day. Maps can show distribution of any information over a geographical location. This could include land elevation information, agricultural information, or demographic information (the numbers of people who can

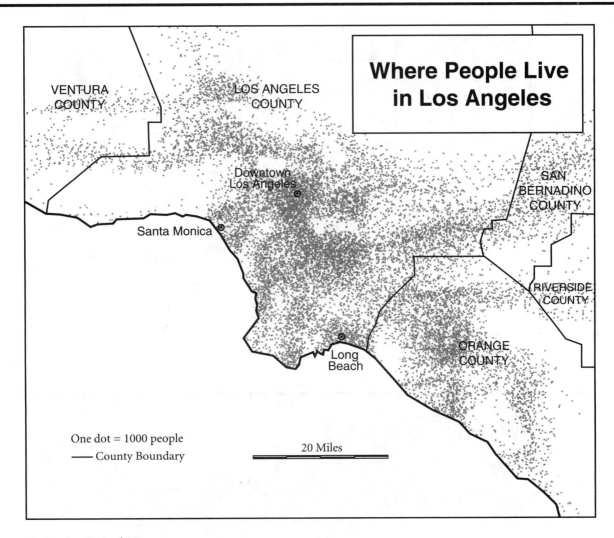

Figure 1.1a. Statistical Map

be described by a specific characteristic such as education level, age, or ethnic background).

The first thing you notice when you look at a map is that it is a picture of a geographical location—a place. After you identify the location, check the title to see what the main purpose is. Then next thing to look for is the type of information displayed on the map; this may be included in the title of the map. When you have identified the geographical location and the type of information that is given, you can mentally make the connection between the place and the data. In other words, the information tells you more about the location pictured on the map.

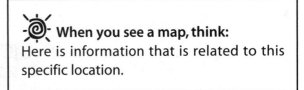

When you see a map, think:
Here is information that is related to this specific location.

The three most common types of maps are statistical maps, descriptive maps, and weather maps.

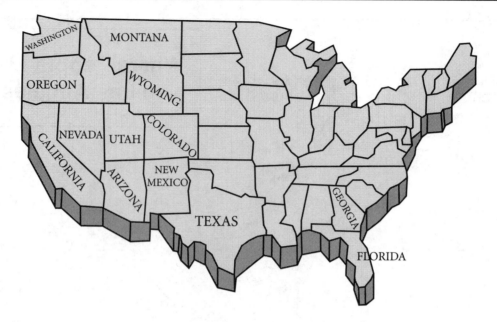

Figure 1.1b. Descriptive Map

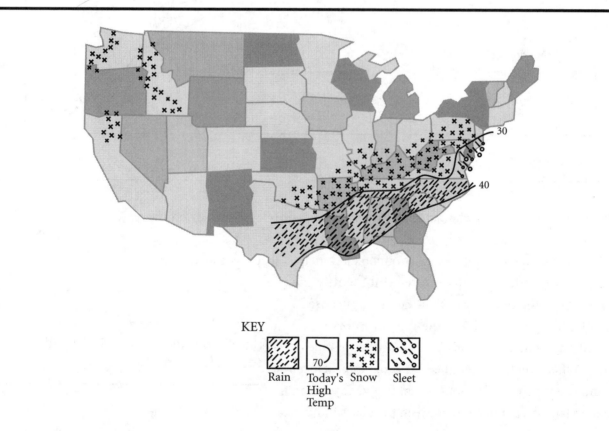

KEY

Rain | Today's High Temp | Snow | Sleet

Figure 1.1c. Weather Map

Type of Education	Description	Typical Time	Where to Get the Training
Course certification	A class that focuses on one piece of software or one technology.	Ranging from half a day to six months	• Temporary agencies • Private training companies • Vendors (the companies that make hardware or software or other technologies)
Program certification	A series of classes that gives an overview of a field.	One to two years	• Vocational schools • Proprietary schools • Independent colleges • Technical schools
Associate degree	Two years of college-level work, with courses in general education and specialized studies.	Two years	• Colleges • Universities • Technical Schools
Bachelor's degree	Four years of college-level work, with courses in general education and a specialized major subject.	Four years	• Colleges • Universities

Figure 1.2. Table

Tables

Tables are one of the most common graphic organizers of information. You will find them in almost every magazine or book that contains facts of any kind. You will use a table to check the batting average of your favorite ball player, or the statistics on your favorite racehorse, or the record of your favorite football player. This format does not illustrate a main idea but simply organizes data into boxes that are easy to read.

> ☼ **When you see a table, think:**
> Here is an organized display of facts that can be read left to right, top to bottom.

A table is easily recognized by its column and row format; it looks a lot like a calendar. Data are organized and lined up vertically and horizontally in squares or cells. Each cell in the top row names the information in the cells below it. The left column of squares or cells contains names of data categories in the rows. Each cell in the left column names the information in the row of cells to the right. The borders on these rows and columns may be displayed or they may not.

							1st &
	Jan	Feb	Mar	Apr	May	June	2nd Qtr
Backwoods School Dist.	$400.00	$400.00	$400.00	$400.00	$400.00	$400.00	$2,400.00
XYZ Company	$300.00	$300.00	$300.00	$300.00	$300.00	$300.00	$1,800.00
M&M Financial Services	$500.00	$500.00	$500.00	$500.00	$500.00	$500.00	$3,000.00
Executive Officers, Inc.	$500.00	$500.00	$500.00	$500.00	$500.00	$500.00	$3,000.00
Main Street Law Office	$400.00	$400.00	$400.00	$400.00	$400.00	$400.00	$2,400.00
Lucky Strike Assoc.			$600.00	$600.00	$600.00	$600.00	$2,400.00
TOTAL	$2,100.00	$2,100.00	$2,700.00	$2,700.00	$2,700.00	$2,700.00	$15,000.00

ULTIMATE SECURITY SERVICES, INC.

1st & 2nd Quarter Income

Figure 1.3. Spreadsheet

Spreadsheets

Spreadsheets are tables with small cells, borders showing, and content that is mostly numbers. They are used for recording, organizing, and handling large quantities of numerical information. Many of the numbers on a spreadsheet are connected, so that if one number changes, other numbers change. This characteristic of spreadsheets makes them useful in predicting financial numbers when one or more cells of information are likely to change. This capability allows a business to predict what the business results will be if certain things happen. This means that they can predict the effect on cash flow and employment levels if product sales fall below the sales forecast—or predict increased quotas per salesperson if a higher sales volume is the target.

> ☀ **When you see a spreadsheet with numerical data, think:**
> Here is financial information. These numbers may be connected. If I change one number, several others will probably change.

This capability is available to all businesses now that computers are common office equipment. Computers give businesses and individuals financial information daily.

Pie Charts

The pie chart is one of the most common graphics used to present data. The idea is easy to understand because most people have had experience with cutting pieces of pie or pizza. A pie chart shows the distribution of more than one piece of a whole entity. For instance, if you counted 100% of citizens who voted in an election, you could show the distribution of votes, according to whom each person

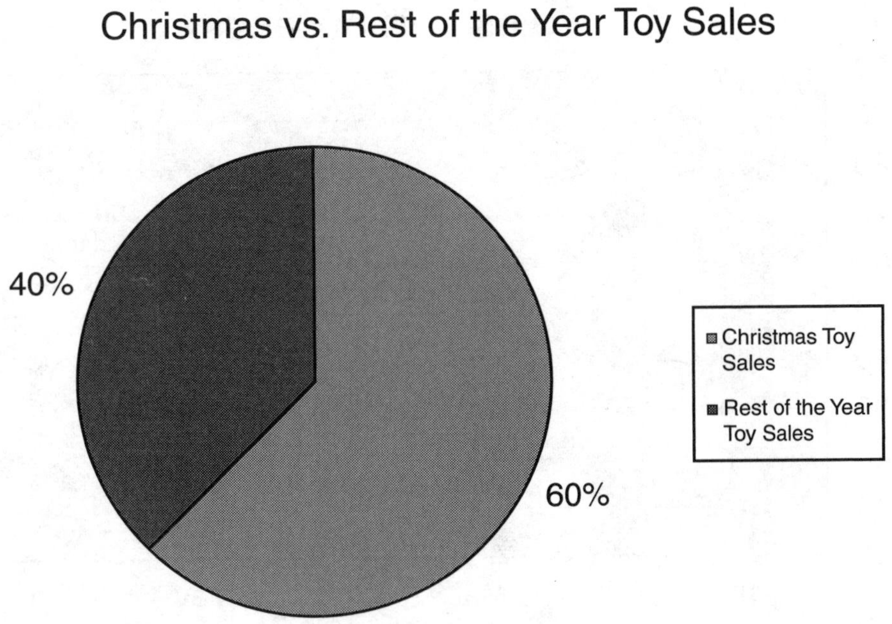

Christmas vs. Rest of the Year Toy Sales

40%

■ Christmas Toy
Sales

■ Rest of the Year
Toy Sales

60%

Figure 1.4. Pie Chart

voted for, on a pie chart. Each segment of the pie chart would equal a certain percentage of the whole pie. You could instantly see which segment of the whole is the largest percentage—just look for the biggest piece of pie.

> **When you see a pie chart, think:** Who, or what, got the biggest piece of the whole pie? Who got the other pieces?

Bar Graphs or Column Graphs

Another common and very popular graph format is the bar graph or column graph. Bar graphs and column graphs are used for many different purposes. You will recognize these graphs right away because they are constructed with several long rectangles to represent the data

> **When you see a bar graph, think:** This shows how these different things relate (or compare) to each other.

categories. These rectangles can either be horizontal (left to right) or vertical (up and down). All the bars on one graph are usually the same width. Bar and column graphs are used to compare several people or things or departments—entities—in a data series.

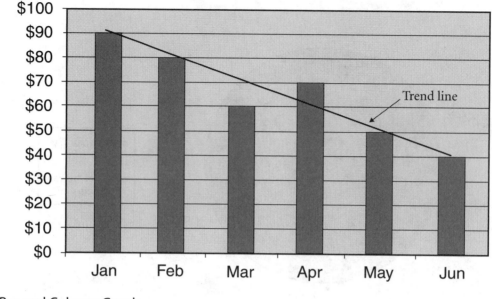

Figure 1.5. Bar and Column Graph

Line Graphs

The line graph is another very common graph that is used for many different purposes. Line graphs show and connect points for a data series such as sales for a month or year, stock value over a specified period of time, or any similar data series for which bar graphs are used. With a quick glance, you can spot high and low times, trends, increase or decrease, and so on. Line graphs appear to draw a mountain range of highs and lows on your chart and make the changes in information very clear.

When you glance at a line graph, you will almost always see one simple fact: it's going either up or down. In order to really understand what the graph indicates, you have to study it further.

> **When you see a line graph, think:** Something is going up or down at different times—or there is a trend one way or another.

Fishbone Diagrams

This graphic gets the award for having the strangest-sounding name, but, when you see it, you will know why. You will always be able to recognize it because it looks like a fish. It is used in problem solving, primarily in quality improvement programs in business. Other names

> **When you see a fishbone diagram, think:** The words written on the head of the fish represent the problem. The words on the ribs of the fish could be causing the problem.

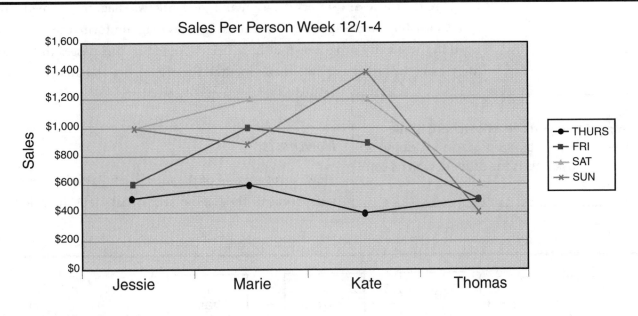

Figure 1.6. Line Graph

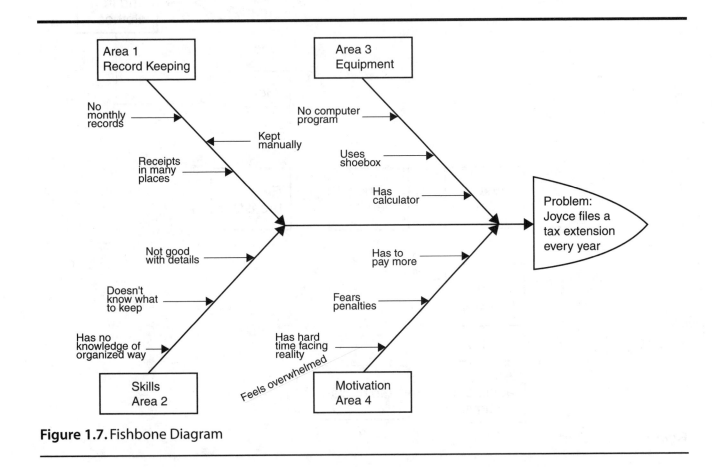

Figure 1.7. Fishbone Diagram

for it are the **cause-and-effect** diagram and the **Ishikawa** diagram (named after Professor Ishikawa of Japan). It is the most famous diagram format to be developed in the quality programs that have been adopted by businesses in the last forty years. It is used as a systematic method for organizing and analyzing data related to solving a quality problem.

> ☀ **When you see a flowchart, think:**
> Here is a step-by-step guide for doing a specific task. This is the order in which I can do it.

Flowcharts

Flowcharts are one of the most useful graphics in business because they show sequential steps in a job or

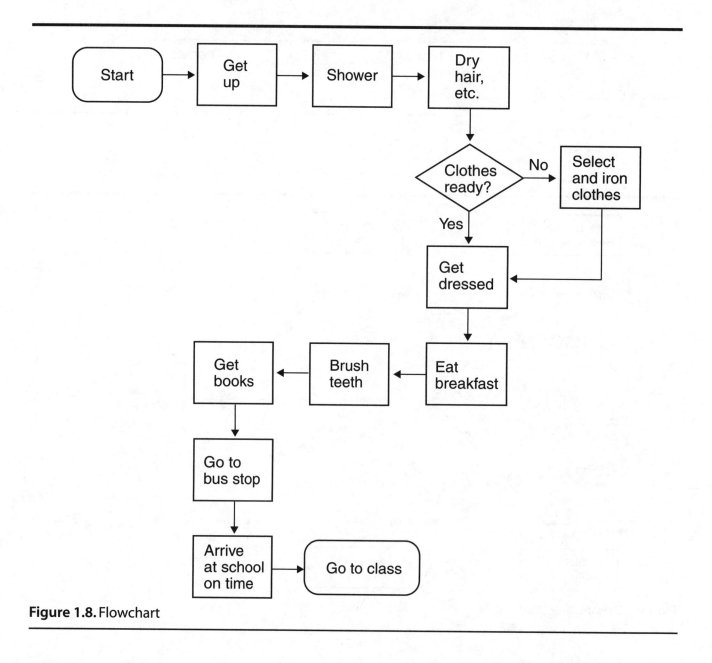

Figure 1.8. Flowchart

process. They are useful for training purposes, for thinking about the necessary steps in a specific process, and as a reference for any worker. Simple flowcharts identify and sequence the major steps in a process.

Tree Diagrams

Tree diagrams show the relationship between main concepts and supporting ideas or contributing factors. Or, as in the family tree, they show an account of a person's or family's ancestry.

> ☀ **When you see a tree diagram, think:** All of the people or things on the branches came from or are related to the first thing on the trunk of the tree.

The tree diagram starts or ends with a main concept which divides into two or more concepts, each of which divides into multiple concepts, and so on. Vertical tree diagrams read from top to bottom. Horizontal tree diagrams read from left to right.

Organization Charts

Any organization that is bigger than a three-person operation could have an organization chart. You can recognize this chart immediately by its format: one

Your father's father Joseph Anthony	*Your father's mother* Carolyn		*Your mother's father* Michael	*Your mother's mother* Charlotte Anne
Your father's siblings Eric Christopher Louis Dianne	*Your father* Matthew		*Your mother* Andrea	*Your mother's siblings* Samuel Jonathan Claire
	You Stephen	*Your siblings* James, Cheryl		

Figure 1.9. Family Tree

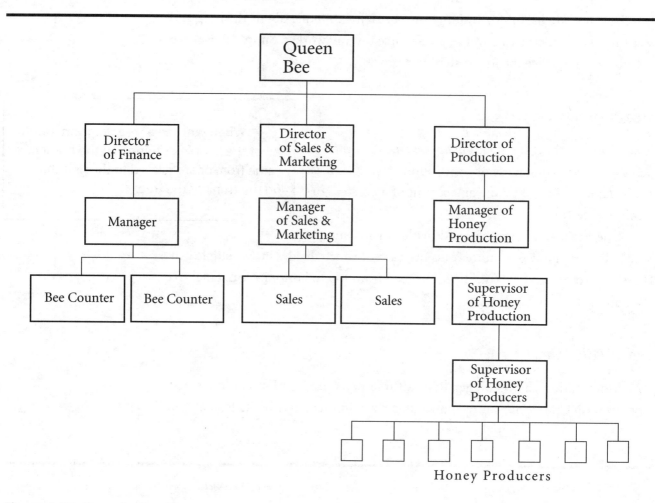

Figure 1.10. Organization Chart

entity (probably) at the top branches out into several levels. Each branch displays a name or position, usually in a rectangular frame. The layout of the organization chart tells you about reporting relationships, or heirarchy, and how far employees are from the decision-makers.

Gantt Charts

Gantt charts are time-management and project-management tools for work groups or individuals. They use the same idea as a timeline to show increments of time and parts of a project that has a definite beginning and end. The main purpose of a Gantt chart is to visually display the different parts of a project in progress and the time frames for each part. This chart gives the participants in the project an idea of who depends on them to get work done and on whom they

Task	Jan	Feb	Mar	April	May
Assessment	▓				
Develop Materials	▓				
Deliver Classes		▓▓▓	▓▓▓	▓▓▓	
Evaluate Program				▓	

Figure 1.11. Gantt Chart

depend for the purpose of meeting project deadlines. It is useful for scheduling, planning, and tracking work on a project when several people are working on it. The Gantt chart is also useful for helping you keep track of several jobs at once.

> ☀ **When you see a Gantt chart, think:** Here is a visual display and schedule of the major parts of a project as they relate to each other.

So there you have it—you've just had a brief overview of the major graphic formats. You'll read more about them, and about their many variations, in the chapters that follow. If you understand the main purpose of each of these formats, you will feel more confident as you interpret the specific information on the graphics.

In the following section, you can use the information you have just read to answer the questions. This will tell you which graphic formats you should go back and review. Answer the questions and then check your answers on page 205.

Check Your Understanding

Use the following graphics to answer the questions below.

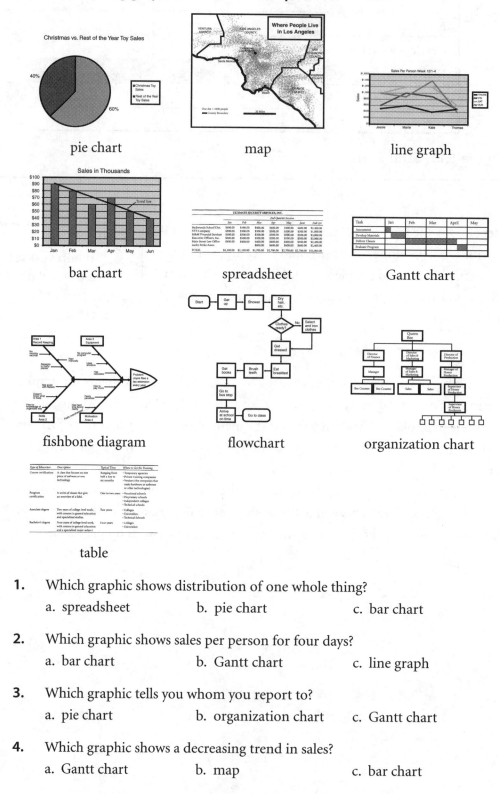

pie chart   map   line graph

bar chart   spreadsheet   Gantt chart

fishbone diagram   flowchart   organization chart

table

1. Which graphic shows distribution of one whole thing?
   a. spreadsheet   b. pie chart   c. bar chart

2. Which graphic shows sales per person for four days?
   a. bar chart   b. Gantt chart   c. line graph

3. Which graphic tells you whom you report to?
   a. pie chart   b. organization chart   c. Gantt chart

4. Which graphic shows a decreasing trend in sales?
   a. Gantt chart   b. map   c. bar chart

5. Which graphic shows the number of people that live in a specific location?

   a. spreadsheet   b. Gantt chart   c. map

6. Which graphic displays numbers that are connected to each other (i.e., if you change one number, other numbers will change)?

   a. spreadsheet   b. line graph   c. bar chart

7. Which graphic shows sequential steps in a task or process?

   a. bar chart   b. pie chart   c. flowchart

8. Circle the main use for the fishbone diagram.

   a. sequencing steps   b. problem solving   c. comparing categories

Your Turn

1. You want to plan a project with a team of people. Each of them works in a different department. You want to clearly identify deadlines for each action step so the final deadline will be achieved. Which graphic tool would you use to display individual responsibilities?

   _____

2. You've been asked to present the results of a survey of 100 people regarding a recall election and their plans to vote. The choices were: Yes—recall, No—don't recall, or U—undecided. Which graphic format would present this information in a quick way with the most impact?

   _____

   _____

Chapter 2

The Key Is the Key

How to Use Titles, Legends, and Measurements to Read Graphics

This chapter will tell you about the special parts of a graphic display that are the keys to unlocking the secrets of each individual graphic. Unlocking this graphic code is the second step in interpreting graphic information. In chapter one, you learned the clues that graphic formats give you. In this chapter, you'll learn to get information from other parts of the graphic.

What Titles, Legends, and Measurements Can Do for You

Graphics can give you a lot of information very quickly if you know what to look for. You will be able to solve the information puzzle that the graphic presents when you know how to interpret the keys. You need to unlock the secrets of certain parts of the graphic before you can interpret the data that is presented. The keys to solving the graphic puzzle are:

- format
- the title of the graphic
- the labels on the parts of the graphic
- the key or legend
- symbols
- scales and tick marks

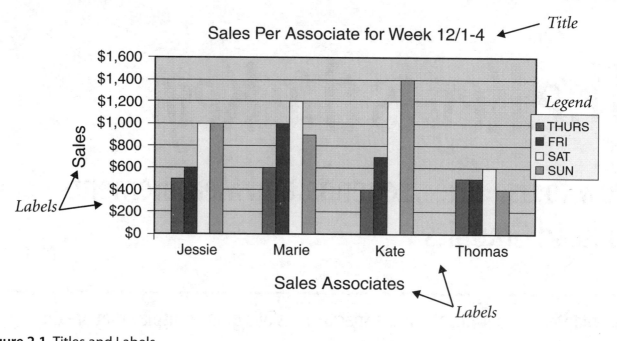

Figure 2.1. Titles and Labels

Titles and Labels

After you have interpreted the main purpose of the graphic, look for large print text that could be a title. The title should tell you the main idea behind the data display. If there is no title, look for other text similar to a caption on a cartoon or photograph in the newspaper. Let the text give you a clue regarding the purpose of the graphic.

Labels will be a few words. You may find them along each of the identified axes. The vertical, or *Y*, axis usually shows you numerical value and the horizontal, or *X*, axis usually names the categories of data. In Figure 2.1 above, the *Y* axis shows a numerical value—the amount of sales. The *X* axis shows the categories, which in this example are the names of the sales associates.

Another use for labels is to identify specific parts or directions on a diagram. Labels are larger than other text and contain few words.

The Key or Legend

One of the best keys to the graphic is the *key* or *legend*. This is a small section on the graphic that displays the special coding of the symbols. Sometimes this coding is color, sometimes it is pattern or size, and sometimes it is different symbols. Most graphics have a key or legend that displays information to help you decode the data graphics.

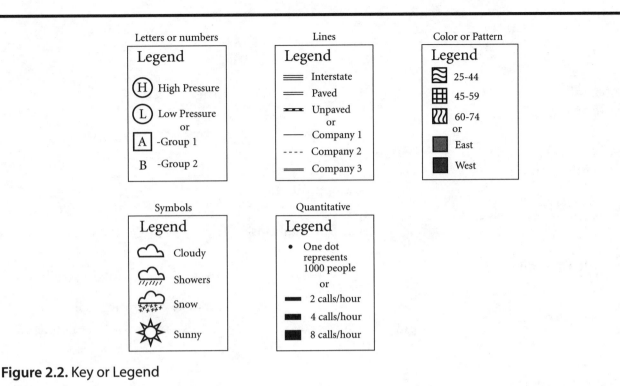

Figure 2.2. Key or Legend

Sometimes a graphic will contain abbreviated versions of labels or explanations. These abbreviated, or shortened, labels are usually explained in the legend of the graphic. Any symbol or text that requires decoding should be referred to in the legend. The legend should clarify anything on the map that is not easily understood.

The main things to look for in a legend are:

- letters, numbers, or abbreviations used to identify categories or other parts of the data
- shadings, patterns, or colors used to identify data series or different characteristics of the data
- symbols that are the same shape but are different in size, which indicate increasing or decreasing quantities
- symbols that stand for places, things, data points, or data series
- type of lines used to represent data series, time frame, or characteristics

Symbols

Symbols are a helpful part of graphics, and the best ones are simple. The line and the arrow are probably two of the most useful symbols; they let you direct your vision in sequential movement on the graphic.

SYMBOLS

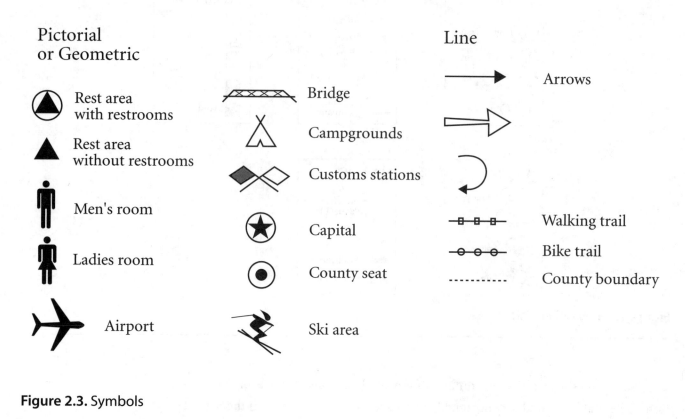

Figure 2.3. Symbols

Dots, triangles, and squares are often used as symbols, as are lines and patterns. When connected to a graphic, the distribution of symbols can tell you a lot about the purpose of the graphic. For instance, a map with a cluster of dots may display population density. After your initial reading of a graphic's format, titles, and labels, go to the legend to decode the symbols.

Scales and Tick Marks

Scales are an orderly system of marks at fixed intervals that indicate measurement quantities. They show an even distribution of information that is similar; usually this distribution is on a line. The most common scale is one of pounds and ounces but there are many other types. The scales that you need to understand for reading graphics are number scales, or extent scales.

The scale that is used for a particular graphic will be displayed somewhere on the graphic. It will probably be in or near the legend.

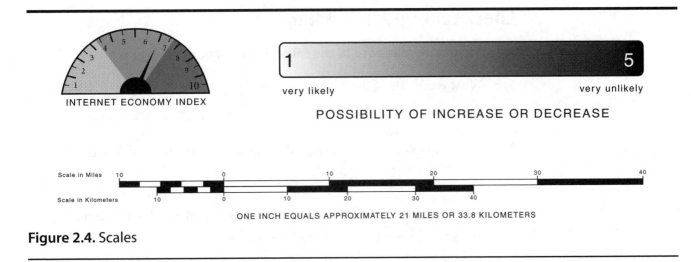

Figure 2.4. Scales

Tick marks are very short lines that are placed crosswise on a longer line or axis. They look like the marks on a ruler. Actually, they make the axis into a ruler or a small measuring tool. They mark off same-size increments on that longer line. They are usually labeled with the type of measurement starting at the lower left-hand corner of a rectangular graph. Each increment is equal to a specific value and the total line is a total of multiples of that specific value. These small increments could be numbers on a quantitative scale, distance on a map scale, or just uniform increments on any scale. The tick marks and their labels are a clue as to how to talk about the numbers that are used to describe the information.

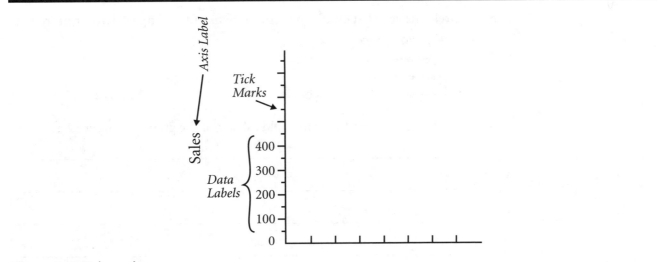

Figure 2.5. Tick marks

Check Your Understanding

Select the correct answer to the following questions.

1. What is the title of the graph in figure 2.1?

   _____

2. On the graph in figure 2.1, find the Y axis. Write the label of this axis here.

   _____

3. Find the data labels on the Y axis of the graph in figure 2.1. Circle the $ value of each segment that is marked by a tick mark.
   a. $100   b. $200   c. $700

4. The legend for the graph in figure 2.1 lists what type of information?
   a. people's names   b. days of the week   c. job duties

5. Circle the symbol that is most likely to stand for rain on a weather map.

   a. ☀   b. ☁   c. 🌧

6. Circle the symbol below that would be the paved freeway if all three symbols were used together.

   a. —   b. ═   c. ═

7. Circle the symbol that would best show several different quantities of a particular thing, such as 5 people, 10 people, and 20 people.

   a. △,△,△   b. ▥, ▨, ▦   c. ○,○,○

8. Circle the set of symbols that could be used to compare two or more persons' performance.

   a.   b. ◐ ● ◑   c. △ △ △

9. Write one question that you could ask about the graphic in figure 2.1.

   _____

   _____

   _____

   _____

Your Turn

Create a small symbol for each of the following items beside their names:

State Highway 18   Fishing

Interstate Freeway 128   Historic Landmark

Dirt Road   Hiking Trail

Paved, Two-Way Road   Museum

Livestock Crossing   Hospital

Ski Slopes   Camping

Place six of the symbols you have created on the following map. Make a legend that explains the symbols.

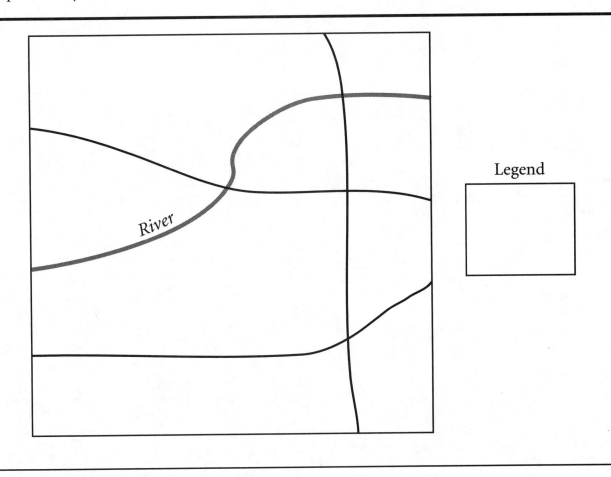

Now you know where to look for the keys to understanding any graphic.

Chapter 3

Beyond Road Maps

Types, Use, and Interpretation of Map Graphics

This chapter examines the most popular graphic display, the map. You are often expected to be able to read maps in your daily activities. In these pages you will learn a method to unlock the mysteries of "geographic data displays"—or maps.

Where You Will Find Them

Maps are a type of graphic you see almost every day. One of the first visual displays of data that you probably remember seeing is the map. You may have used a map to display information about agriculture or exports in social studies assignments in elementary school. Maps are introduced at this age because they are useful in connecting information to a geographical location. They let you quickly compare data for one geographical location to the data for another location. These data could refer to density of population, weather conditions, agricultural production, or any other appropriate topic.

In a foreign country, maps are helpful guides even if you don't speak the language. Basic layouts of maps, including directions and symbols, can be understood without mastery of the written language. Reading maps is a useful skill that you will find handy for the rest of your life.

Maps are usually one of the following:

- descriptive maps
- weather maps
- statistical maps

> **When you see a map, think:**
> Here is information that is related to this specific location.

Descriptive Maps

Sometimes maps are descriptive and tell you something about an area, such as where the museums, libraries, airports, and sports facilities are located. Sometimes they tell you which roads are freeways and which are two-way roads. Sometimes they give you rapid transit routes and other helpful information. The map in figure 3.1 shows small pictures of popular tourist attractions in Rome. The legend explains the symbols that are used to indicate popular tourist attractions. This type of map is easy for a foreigner to follow.

Weather Maps

Television news programs show weather maps several times a day. No doubt you often look at the weather map and tune out the weather person because the map tells you temperatures, weather conditions, or air quality at a glance. You could be listening to your favorite CD and still figure out whether or not to take your umbrella to work.

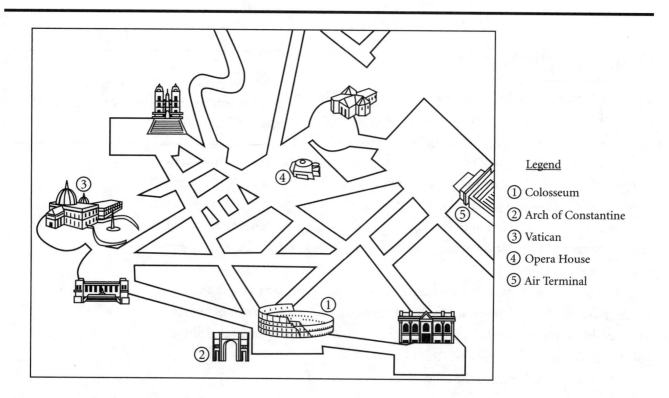

Figure 3.1. Descriptive Map

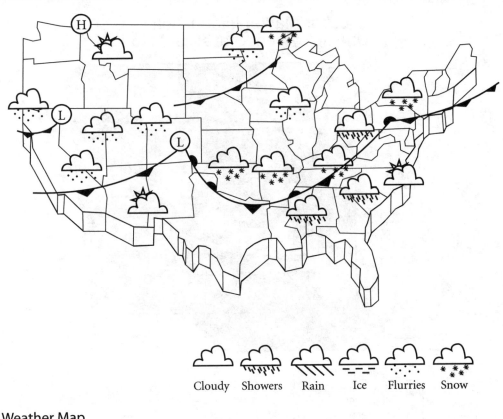

Cloudy   Showers   Rain   Ice   Flurries   Snow

Figure 3.2. Weather Map

If you miss the TV news program, you can pick up the newspaper and turn to the weather column. With one look, you can see what the weather is like in another time zone. You will know to pack your boots if it will be snowing in Chicago when you get off the plane.

A weather map shows the different forms of weather occurring in a broad location, such as the United States, at a specific time. On the weather map you can quickly see where the thunderstorms will be and where the rain will turn to snow. This can be useful for:

- planning travel—What should you pack? Should you go at all?
- communicating with family or friends—you can talk about the storm, or the sunshine
- understanding other types of situations affected by the weather
  —beach conditions
  —ski conditions

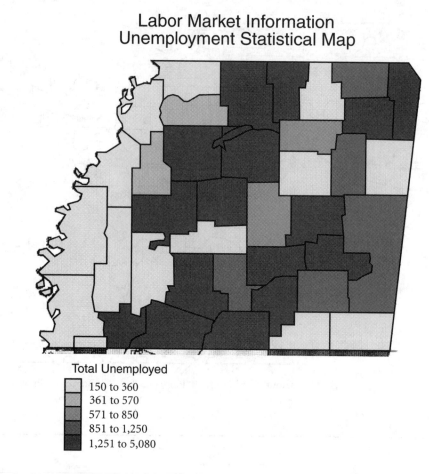

Figure 3.3. Statistical Map

Statistical Maps

Statistical maps are maps that show quantitative information about locations, distances, or areas. They are constructed by using a map of an area and placing quantitative information on it. Usually, the map is rather plain with only the most important geographical details showing. For instance, the county or state borders might show but most of the cities would not. The map is drawn as a background for the data.

What to Look For

World maps are characterized by grid lines that divide the geographic area in question into chunks. Maps of large bodies of land and water, or maps of the world, have latitude and longitude lines that divide the mapped area into chunks. Parallel lines or latitudes run east and west. Meridian lines or longitudes run

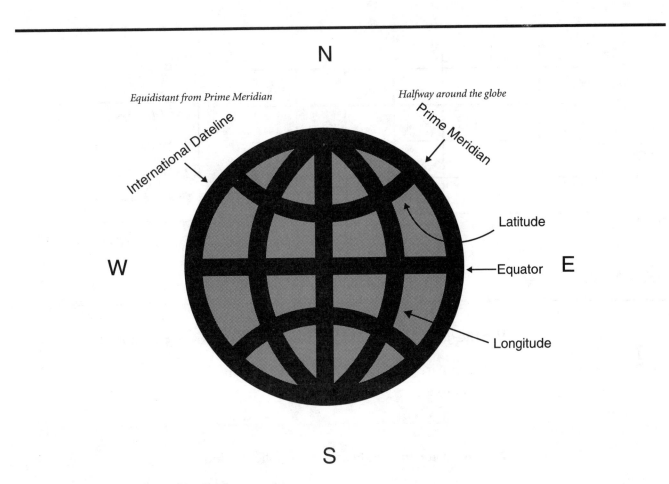

Figure 3.4. Longitude and Latitude

north and south. Parallels measure distances north and south of the Equator and are parallel to it. Meridians measure distances east and west from the prime meridian. Halfway around the globe at the 180-degree meridian, these measurements meet, and at that point the meridian is called the International Date Line. When navigators cross the International Date Line they add or drop a day. East of this line is one day earlier than west of the line. Consequently, going east they drop a day, and going west they add a day.

Most statistical maps and descriptive maps will not have longitude and latitude lines on them but you will see them on maps that represent a larger area.

Coordinates

Maps of smaller areas, such as sections of a city or state, are organized by coordinates which are very similar to longitude and latitude lines. These coordinates, or gridlines, can help you find very specific addresses on maps as well as broader locations. They break unfamiliar territory into manageable chunks of information.

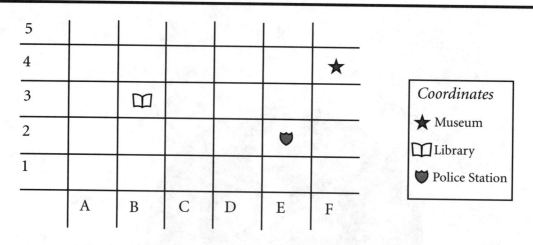

Figure 3.5. Coordinates

Use the graphics in figure 3.5 to answer the following questions.

1.   If F,4 are the coordinates of the museum, what are the coordinates of the library?

_____

2.   What are the coordinates of the police station?

_____

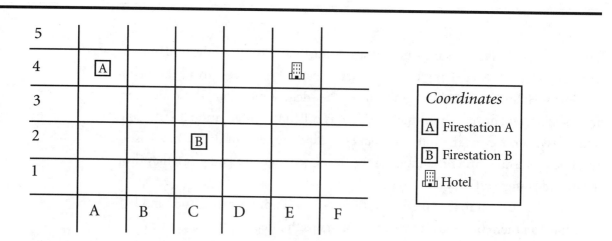

Figure 3.6. Coordinates

Use the graphics in figure 3.6 to answer the following question.

1.   You are staying in a hotel shown on the diagram above. A fire breaks out on the floor above you and you call the fire department. A fire engine is dis-

patched from the nearest fire station. Which of the stations shown above is the nearest to your hotel?

_____

_____

Steps to Reading a Map

1. Identify the Location

Unless the location is well known to everyone who sees the map, it should be labeled. It will have a title either at the top of a label or on the area that is mapped.

2. Find the Key

A key or legend will help you unlock the information that is unique to the map you are studying. The legend should define the use of symbols and scales for that

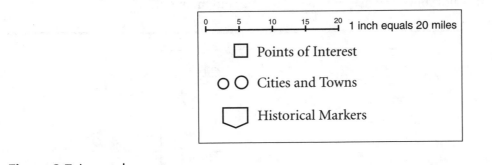

Figure 3.7. Legend

particular map. It is found toward the bottom of the map or over to one side. Sometimes it is labeled "Legend" and sometimes it has no label at all.

3. Check the Symbols

Some symbols—such as the arrow—always mean the same thing and are not defined for each map. Any graphic symbols that are used to show specific information for the map you are interpreting should be defined in the map legend.

Symbols are small graphic representations of data that you can quickly understand. The most common symbols are points (geometrical and pictorial) and lines.

Points:

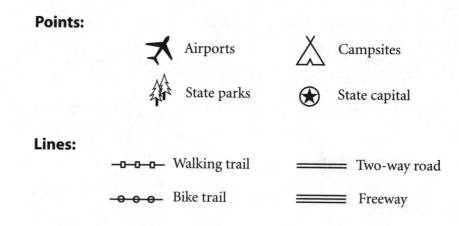

Lines:

▫▫▫	Walking trail	══	Two-way road
⊙⊙⊙	Bike trail	≡	Freeway

4. Check the Scales

No, not the ones used for determining your weight! We mean scales that are used for recording and understanding information on maps. A distance scale is to show how far it is from one place to another. Graphic scales are correct even when the map has been enlarged or reduced on a copier.

  Some useful graphic scales are bar scales and elevation scales.

Bar scales

Bar scales show distance and give you a measurement guide.

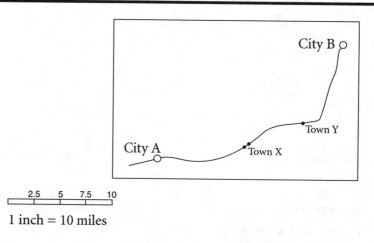

Figure 3.8. Using a Scale

Use the graphic in figure 3.8 to answer the following question.

1. According to the above map, about how far is it from City A to City B if one travels in a straight line?

Elevation Scales

Elevation scales show land elevation or variations of any descriptive characteristic by color or pattern.

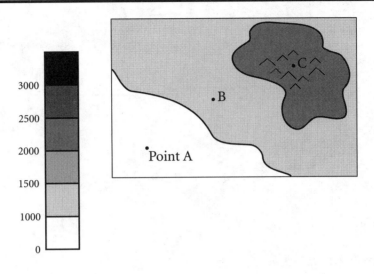

Figure 3.9. Elevation Scales

Use the graphic in figure 3.9 to answer the following questions.

1. What is the elevation at point C?

_____

2. How much higher is point C than point B?

_____

Your Turn

On the map on the next page, show the following information:

George Towne has a successful seafood restaurant in San Diego, California. He has decided to open other restaurants in California and the United States. To make it easy to see the distance between his restaurants, he wants to mark the planned restaurants on a map using 🍴 as a symbol. Help George see his expansion plan by drawing symbols on the map in these quantities:

3 restaurants in San Diego   1 restaurant in Los Angeles

4 restaurants in San Francisco   1 restaurant in Texas

1 restaurant in Florida   1 restaurant in Maine

1 restaurant in Chicago

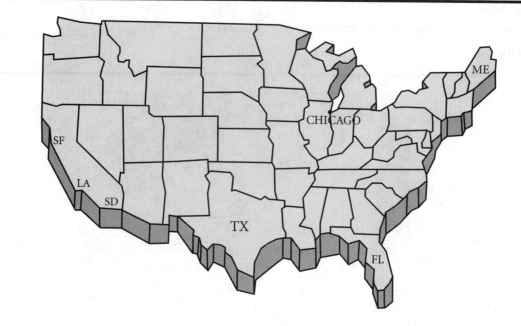

Figure 3.10. George's Seafood Restaurants

Congratulations! You and George can now visualize his restaurant chain on a national level.

Chapter 4

Keeping Track of Information

Checksheets, Logs, and Tables

Sometimes graphics serve as tools to record and organize information as it is gathered, and for keeping that information organized until decisions are made about it. Tools that do this are called *checksheets* and *logs*. In this chapter, you will learn to use these tools in your daily activities.

Where You Will Find Them

Checksheets, logs, and tables are common and useful tools for gathering and organizing facts. Checksheets and logs are used more for gathering information while tables are used for displaying data. Checksheets and logs are found on every business manager's desk, on the wall, and under a pile of other work. Tables are found in almost every magazine and paper. Each of these graphic tools is similar to the other two: each is constructed by drawing several *rows* (two horizontal lines) perpendicular to several *columns* (two vertical lines).

CHECKSHEET FOR THE WEEK OF				
Nov. 4-6				

Department				
Molding				

DEFECTS	Monday	Tuesday	Wednesday	TOTAL
Bubbles	ЖТ I	ЖТ ЖТ	ЖТ ЖТ ЖТ II	
Spray	ЖТ ЖТ ЖТ	III	ЖТ	
Short Shot	ЖТ ЖТ ЖТ ЖТ ЖТ II	ЖТ ЖТ ЖТ ЖТ ЖТ ЖТ II	ЖТ ЖТ ЖТ ЖТ ЖТ ЖТ ЖТ II	

Forklift Pre-Use Checksheet

☐ Fire Extinguisher— Present and Charged

☐ Engine Oil Level

☐ Fuel Level

☐ Radiator Water Level

☐ Note any damage, loose or missing bolts, nuts, guards, chains, hydraulic hose reel

☐ Wheels/Tires— tread OK, tires round

☐ Forks— positioning latches in working order, carriage teeth not broken, chipped or worn

☐ Anchor Pins on Chains— Pins not worn, loose, or bent

☐ Fluid leaks— Damp spots or drips of fluid may indicate a leak

☐ Battery— Cables (no exposed wires); Water level— record water added

☐ Hoses— Held securely, not loose or rubbing

Figure 4.1. Checksheets

Checksheets

Checksheets are generally used for recording activities. Their exact purpose varies: Sometimes their purpose is to record frequency—show how many times something happens. Sometimes they are a list of things to do, like the ever-popular "To Do" list. In the workplace, the checksheet may list the steps for starting up or shutting down a machine or for completing a process. Each step is checked off as it is done. This type of checksheet could also be used for opening or closing a store or department. Checksheets are especially useful in situations where you are new to the job and you need to make sure every step is followed.

> ☼ **When you see a checksheet, think:** Here is record of how often these things are happening.

When the checksheet is used for recording frequency, items that could be recorded include defects (as in figure 4.1), customer complaints, loss of cable service, or many other things. These things are usually counted individually, as with *hatch* marks or *slash* marks, one at a time. At the end of a specific time period, you can count the marks and summarize the data.

Once the data are summarized, you can study them and try to determine what they mean. Does one defect happen more than the others? Are there more defects on a particular day? A particular hour? This information helps you make a decision about which defect should be investigated further.

Keep Track of Your Sales Performance

You can use a checksheet to keep track of your on-the-job performance. The simple checksheet below is a good way to keep track of your own sales if you work in a retail store. With this tool, you can quickly make a slash mark every time you make a sale. The purpose of this is to keep your personal record of how you are doing. Sales managers have found that people who keep a record of their sales performance increase their sales very quickly. If your salary is tied to your sales in any way, this can be a great motivator. One reason we like to play sports is we always know what the score is, thanks to a scoreboard. Keeping track of your own productivity this way helps you set and reach your own goals. Keeping track of your sales is sure to impress any sales manager!

Sales Checksheet for		Tess Roberts			
Dates		_____			
$ Amount	**Thurs**	**Fri**	**Sat**	**Sun**	**Total**
Under $10	~~卌~~ ~~卌~~	////	////	~~卌~~ ~~卌~~	28
$10 - $50	~~卌~~ ~~卌~~ ~~卌~~ ~~卌~~ ~~卌~~ ~~卌~~	~~卌~~ ~~卌~~ ~~卌~~ ~~卌~~ ~~卌~~ ~~卌~~	~~卌~~ ~~卌~~ ~~卌~~ ~~卌~~ ~~卌~~ ~~卌~~	~~卌~~ ~~卌~~ ~~卌~~ ~~卌~~ ~~卌~~ ~~卌~~ ~~卌~~ ~~卌~~	145
$50 - $100	~~卌~~ ~~卌~~ //	~~卌~~ ~~卌~~ ~~卌~~ ~~卌~~ ~~卌~~ //	~~卌~~ ~~卌~~ ~~卌~~ ~~卌~~ ~~卌~~ ~~卌~~ ~~卌~~	~~卌~~ ~~卌~~	84
Over $100	—	//	////	/	6
Total					
	52	58	77	76	263

Figure 4.2. Sales Checksheet

Use the checksheet in figure 4.2 to answer the following questions.

1. In which price range were most of Tess' sales?
    a. $50–$100   b. Under $10   c. $10–$50

2. On which day did Tess have largest total sales?
    a. Thursday   b. Sunday   c. Saturday

3. On which day did Tess sell the least?
    a. Thursday   b. Sunday   c. Friday

4. If Tess could earn a commission (percent of sales) on her sales, which price range should she focus on increasing?
    a. $50–$100   b. under $10   c. over $100

Team Problem Solving: Safety Shoe Checksheet

You begin the process of translating opinions into facts with the checksheet. For example, if your work team thinks that workers on your shift are not wearing safety shoes, you can record the actual times this happens by doing the following things:

1. Decide what to count.

Say you decide to make a hatch mark for each worker not wearing safety shoes. You don't write the names down. Just count the times it happens. You have to be careful to record the behavior, not the person. Otherwise, no one will cooperate with you.

2. Decide on the span of time to be measured.

For this example, a specific number of days and hours would work.

3. Create a checksheet that will be easy to use.

4. Record data consistently and honestly.

CHECKSHEET FOR THE WEEK OF 1st Shift		3/1 - 3		
Department	Large Motor Assembly			
Safety shoe noncompliance	Monday	Tuesday	Wednesday	
Standard Safety	IIII	ЖЖ	ЖЖ I	
Athletic Shoes	ЖЖ ЖЖ ЖЖ ЖЖ	ЖЖ ЖЖ III	ЖЖ ЖЖ ЖЖ	
Leather Soles Sturdy Body	ЖЖ I	ЖЖ ЖЖ II	ЖЖ IIII	
Flimsy Body	III	ЖЖ I	ЖЖ	

Figure 4.3. Safety Shoe Checksheet

Logs

Logs are tools for recording the names of specific people using a machine or working in an area at a specific time. You log on to a computer. That means you sign on and give your password, which automatically records who was using the computer and in what time frame. You may have to log in when you begin working on a specific machine either in the office or in the operations area of a business. A log is also used for recording amounts of work performed by a specific person at a specific time.

> -☉- **When you see a log, think:**
> Here is record of everyone who worked on this and exactly how much work they did or when they did it.

SAMPLE LOG

Production Log for Molding Machine 6066

Product	Beginning	Ending	Operator	Total Produced	Supervisor
Part #2436a	65,450	66,950	Ralph	1,500	*MDD*
Part #4059b	42,200	44,200	Charlie	2,000	
Part #5689a	6,890	8,025	Sharon	1,135	*LH*
Total	**114,540**	**119,175**		**4,635**	

Figure 4.4. Production Log

Use the log in figure 4.4 to answer the following questions.

1. What was the beginning inventory count when Charlie logged on to the machine?

   _____

2. What was Ralph's total production?

   _____

3. Which operator did not get his/her supervisor to sign off on his numbers?

   _____

Pictographs

The pictograph is a graph that is similar to the checksheet. The difference is that the pictograph uses a picture instead of a table format. You may think that a pictograph is a graph that uses symbols for the data quantities, or maybe you think it is a drawing on the wall of a cave. It could be either of those things, but in the work place, it's more likely to be a drawing of a product. This picture is used for recording defects. It is a simple, clear way of recording these defects and is very easy to read. The reader can visualize the product with its numerous defects at a glance.

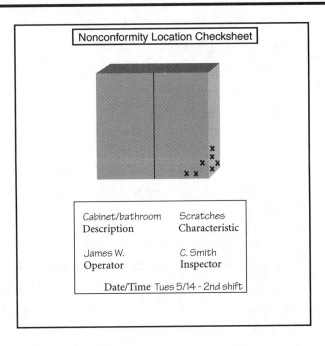

Figure 4.5. Nonconformity Location Checksheet

Use the pictograph in figure 4. 5 to answer the following questions.

1. What is the name of the product?

   _____

2. Who is the machine operator?

   _____

3. How many defects are there on the product?

   _____

4. Why is this a good way to record defects?

   _____

Tables

Tables are the graphic organizers that you see every day in newspapers, magazines, business windows, sports scorecards, bus schedules, and on and on. Tables may look a lot like checksheets and logs, but they have a different job to do. Checksheets and logs are forms that are used for gathering information—recording facts as they happen. Tables are used for displaying information—summarizing those specific facts and organizing them so you can read them in rows (left to right) or in columns (top to bottom).

> ☀ **When you see a table, think:**
> Here is an organized display of facts that can be read left to right, top to bottom.

To interpret a table:

1. Find and read:
    *   the title
    *   the labels on the columns
    *   the labels on the rows

2. Follow the first column of labels on the left with your finger. Find the label for the information you want and move your finger from left to right in that row. Keep your finger right on that row. Use figure 4.6 below to practice and find the information for August 25.

3. Next, find the information label in the top row that names the information you want. In figure 4.6, choose **Number**. Follow that column from top to bottom with your right hand. Bring your left hand across the August 25 row at the same time. The place where your row and column come together is the information you are looking for.

	Date	Time	Place	Number	Type	Rate	Minutes	Amount
			Julie's August Long-Distance Phone Bill					
1.	Aug23	10:35pm	Covina, CA	626 814-0218	Direct	Night	9	.09
2.	Aug24	8:28pm	Covina, CA	626 856-0940	Direct	Eve	18	.90
3.	Aug24	9:07pm	Atlanta, GA	404 310-6534	Direct	Eve	15	2.25
4.	Aug25	2:30am	SnFrncsco, CA	415 615-3072	Direct	Night	8	.40
5.	Aug26	10:30am	SnFrncsco, CA	415 615-3072	Direct	Day	10	1.20
6.	Aug27	12:00pm	Riverside, CA	909 564-9502	Direct	Night	22	1.76
Total							**82**	**$6.60**

Figure 4.6. Julie's August Long-Distance Phone Bill

Use the table in figure 4. 6 to answer the following questions.

1. What was the city that Julie called on August 26?
   a. Atlanta   b. San Francisco   c. Riverside

2. What was the rate for the August 26 phone call?
   a. Day   b. Night   c. Direct

3. How many long-distance calls did Julie make during the week shown on the table?
   a. ten   b. two   c. six

4. Which call cost the most?
   a. #5   b. #3   c. #6

5. How many long-distance minutes did Julie use in August? _____

6. What was the total cost of these six phone calls?_____

Your Turn

You will see how useful these tools are if you learn to use them yourself. First, choose something to count, such as how many tables in a bookstore coffee shop are taken by people who are reading at the tables and not buying anything. It would be useful to select the hours for the survey, such as 1:00 p.m.–3:00 p.m. If you did that every day for a week, you would have an idea how the tables were being used. You might want to count empty tables, tables with customers eating, tables with customers drinking one cup of coffee while reading magazines or working, and tables with customers reading or working and not buying anything.

For this exercise, take the following information and record it on the check-sheet provided. (If you have time, go to a bookstore and do this exercise, counting actual people.) Then organize it into a table so it can be easily read.

The local bookstore has a coffee bar that has eleven tables for seating. People sit for hours at the tables reading the magazines and studying without buying food or coffee or without continuing to purchase food after they have been there for an hour or so. The problem is that there is no seating for customers who do want to buy food and the coffee bar is losing money. Matthew, the manager, has decided to study the situation before changing any of the coffee bar policies about the tables. He recorded data for four 1:00 p.m.–3:00 p.m. and the following is what he found.

- Monday there were eight tables used by 16 people studying, no purchase in sight. Three customers eating lunch were using two tables, and one table was empty.

- Tuesday there were 14 people studying at seven tables, six people eating at three tables, and one person working at one table with an empty coffee mug on the table.
- Wednesday there were 14 people studying at eight tables, one person eating at one table, and two people at two tables with empty coffee mugs on the table.
- Thursday there were 11 people, one person at each table reading. Three of the tables have coffee cups on them and one table has food trays on it.

CHECKSHEET

Number of People and Table Usage at the Caffeine Club
Time: 1:00 p.m.–3:00 p.m. daily

Table Usage	Monday People / Tables	Tuesday People/ Tables	Wednesday People /Tables	Thursday People/ Tables	Total People/ Tables
Reading/Working Dirty dishes					
Food customer					
Person studying/ No food					
Empty tables					

After recording the data on the checksheet, organize the data into the table below.

TABLE

Number of People and Table Usage at the Caffeine Club
Time: 1:00 p.m.–3:00 p.m. daily

Table Usage	Monday People/Tables	Tuesday People/Tables	Wednesday People/Tables	Thursday People/Tables	Total People/Tables
Reading/Working Dirty dishes					
Food customer					
Person studying/ No food					
Empty tables					

Great work! You and Matthew now have some facts recorded that will help him decide what to do about the table usage problems in the coffee shop. He now has more than a feeling or an opinion. He has what we call *hard data*—an actual record of table usage as he observed it between 1:00 p.m.–3:00 p.m. on four week days. He is one step closer to solving his problem because he has made it visible and quantifiable.

Chapter 5

Crunching Numbers

Spreadsheets

In this chapter you will learn about a useful business tool, the spreadsheet. Now, instead of running when you see one of these sheets full of numbers, you will be able to decipher it quickly and easily.

Where You Will Find Them

Spreadsheets are the structural skeleton of the business plan. They are useful for predicting financial numbers as well as checking them. Every accounting department uses computer-generated spreadsheets. As other departments in a business become responsible for financial improvements and controls, more and more department managers create their department spreadsheets and they are all expected to read them. Every small business should use a spreadsheet for planning and predicting as well as reporting numbers for the business.

> ☼ **When you see a spreadsheet, think:** Here is financial information. These numbers may be interconnected. If I change one number, several others will probably change.

The spreadsheet is organized a lot like a table. The top row contains the column titles. The far left column contains the labels for the rows. Each small rectangle in the spreadsheet is called a cell. Each cell contains specific information. You read the spreadsheet from top to bottom and from left to right, the same way you read tables.

While spreadsheets can be calculated manually, their real value lies in the fact that they can be created and changed quickly when they are done on a computer. This ease of handling and creating spreadsheets has made them a widely used

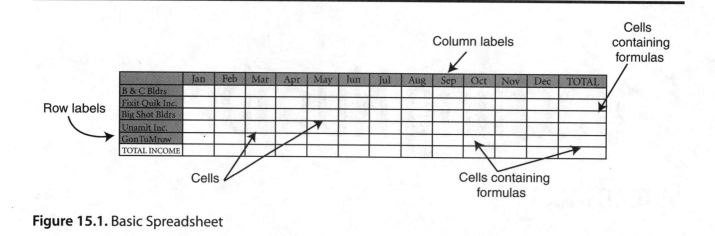

Figure 15.1. Basic Spreadsheet

business financial tool. In the spreadsheet in figure 5.1, the column labeled "Total" calculates the amount automatically. The row labeled "Total Income" also does automatic calculation.

To read a spreadsheet, you don't *have* to understand where the numbers came from, but it is helpful if you do. The secret to the changing numbers on a spreadsheet is the formulas that exist in the cells. These formulas are mathematical calculations. So, the person who creates the formulas for the different cells and functions of the spreadsheet has to understand the formulas, but *you* don't necessarily have to. Frequently all you have to do is just fill in the numbers and the computer will do the rest. All you have to do is know how to interpret it.

You can use spreadsheets when you want to calculate interest payment on a loan, or when you want to see how much of your loan payment is going to the actual loan and how much of it is going to pay the interest on the loan. In the following spreadsheets, interest on a loan has been figured with two different interest rates. Once the spreadsheet is created, with all of its formulas in place, you can simply change the interest rate and all of the other figures will be re-figured for you. What a time saver!

Comparing Interest Rates

Sol and Nancy are considering taking out a loan for some home improvements and they have two different loan opportunities. One loan has a 9% variable interest rate which could go up at any time, with no cap on it. The other loan is with their credit union where they are known. It has a 12% fixed interest rate. They want to decide whether to take a chance and go with the lower rate or to stay with their credit union for the fixed rate.

Home Improvement Loan #1

Date	Pmt	Principal	Interest	Balance
			9%	6,600.00
1/6/99	1	295.50	49.50	6,304.50
2/6/99	2	297.72	47.28	6,006.78
3/6/99	3	299.95	45.05	5,704.60
4/6/99	4	302.20	42.80	5,404.63
5/6/99	5	304.47	40.53	5,100.16
6/6/99	6	306.75	38.25	4,793.41
7/6/99	7	309.05	35.95	4,484.36
8/6/99	8	311.37	33.63	4,170.76
9/6/99	9	313.70	31.30	3,859.29
10/6/99	10	316.06	28.94	3,543.23
11/6/99	11	318.43	26.57	3,224.80
12/6/99	12	320.81	24.19	2,903.99
	Total Paid	3375.20	419.89	

Home Improvement Loan #2

Date	Pmt	Principal	Interest	Balance
			12%	6,600.00
1/6/99	1	279.00	66.00	6,321.00
2/6/99	2	281.79	63.21	6,039.21
3/6/99	3	284.61	60.39	5,751.78
4/6/99	4	287.48	57.52	5,467.12
5/6/99	5	290.33	54.67	5,176.79
6/6/99	6	293.23	51.77	4,883.56
7/6/99	7	296.16	48.84	4,587.39
8/6/99	8	299.13	45.87	4,285.45
9/6/99	9	302.15	42.85	3,986.12
10/6/99	10	305.14	39.86	3,680.98
11/6/99	11	308.19	36.81	3,372.79
12/6/99	12	311.27	33.73	3,061.52
	Total Paid	3538.48	601.52	

Figure 5.2. Home Improvement Loan Rates

Use the spreadsheets in figure 5.2 to answer the following questions.

1. At the end of one year, using the 9% interest rate, how much will they have paid on the principal of the loan?

   _____

2. How much will they have paid in interest on the 9% loan?

   _____

3. At the end of one year, using the 12% interest rate, how much will they have paid on the principal of the loan?

   _____

4. How much will they have paid in interest on the 12% loan?

   _____

5. Which loan shows the most money paid on the principal?

   _____

6. Which loan shows the most money paid in interest?

   _____

7. How much is the difference paid in interest for one year?

   _____

Now the decision about the loan is up to Sol and Nancy. They have the facts.

Jameson Family Expenses and Income

The Jameson family has planned their income and expenses for the next six months because they want to keep their expenses in line and have a "cushion" in case of emergencies. If the extra is not spent on necessities, they want to put it aside for a vacation. The spreadsheet in figure 5.3a shows the projected income/expenses for six months. The spreadsheet in figure 5.3b shows the "what-if" projection. It includes:

- What if the rent goes up?
- What if we spend more on food?
- What if our health insurance premium increases?
- What if we increase our business income?

Use the spreadsheets in figure 5.3 to answer the following questions.

1. In what month did the rent increase?
   a. January   b. February   c. March

Jameson Family Expenses and Income

Expense	Jan	Feb	Mar	Apr	May	June	Total
Rent	800	800	800	800	800	800	4800
Food	400	400	400	400	400	400	2400
Car	259	259	259	259	259	259	1554
Car Ins.	125	125	125	125	125	125	750
Health Ins.	186	186	186	186	186	186	1116
Life Ins.	56	56	56	56	56	56	336
Clothes	150	150	150	150	150	150	900
Entertain	150	150	150	150	150	150	900
Misc.	200	200	200	200	300	400	1500
Savings	100	100	100	100	100	100	600
Total	**2426**	**2426**	**2426**	**2426**	**2526**	**2626**	**14856**
Income							
Contract 1	1800	1800	1800	1800	1800	1800	10800
Contract 2	1200	1200	1200	1200	1200	1200	7200
Total	**3000**	**3000**	**3000**	**3000**	**3000**	**3000**	**18000**
Cushion	574	574	574	574	474	374	3144

Figure 5.3a. Projected Income/Expenses

Jameson Family Expenses and Income

Expense	Jan	Feb	Mar	Apr	May	June	Total
Rent	800	900	900	900	900	900	5300
Food	400	400	450	450	450	450	2600
Car	259	259	259	259	259	259	1554
Car Ins.	125	125	125	125	125	125	750
Health Ins.	186	186	226	226	226	226	1276
Life Ins.	56	56	56	56	56	56	336
Clothes	150	150	150	150	150	150	900
Entertain	150	150	150	150	150	200	950
Misc.	200	200	200	200	300	400	1500
Savings	100	100	100	100	100	100	600
Total	**2426**	**2526**	**2616**	**2616**	**2716**	**2866**	**15766**
Income							
Contract 1	1800	1800	1800	1800	1800	1800	10800
Contract 2	1200	1200	1200	1200	1200	1200	7200
New Bus.				600	600	600	1800
Total	**3000**	**3000**	**3000**	**3600**	**3600**	**3600**	**19800**
Cushion	574	474	384	984	884	734	4034

Figure 5.3b. What-If Scenario

2. Did any other expense increase that month?

   _____

3. When did other expenses increase?
   a. February   b. March   c. April

4. What did the Jamesons do to increase the "cushion" against unexpected expenses?
   a. saved more money   b. spent less   c. increased business income

You can also use a spreadsheet to keep track of your checkbook. You just enter the information into the spreadsheet—just like you would in your check register—and the spreadsheet does the adding and subtracting for you. It will also do some other tricky things behind the scenes, if you enter the correct formulas. In figure 5.4, you have a copy of the Jameson family's check register. Again, like a table, the column labels are entered from left to right in the first row of the spreadsheet. You enter the dates when you write the checks, from top to bottom in the first column on the left. In the next column, the number of the check is written. Read about the transaction from left to right, across the row. Computerized financial programs will do all of this for you when you write a check, which is then printed out. The program then enters the information into the check register and does all of the calculating for you.

In the second row of the spreadsheet in figure 5.4, you see the date December 31. Then there is no information until you get to the last column—marked *balance*. The balance is the amount that is in the bank account on that day. Then the check amounts are subtracted out of the balance and the deposits are added in.

Use the spreadsheet in figure 5.4 to answer the following questions.

1. What was the balance in the checking account on December 31?

   _____

2. On what day was the first deposit of payment from contract 1 deposited?

   _____

3. Did the Jamesons pay their health insurance? _____

   On what day was it paid? _____

4. What is the balance in the account on January 31?

   _____

5. Was the car payment check written before January 10? _____

Jameson Family Check Register

Date	Check#	Item	Deposit	Withdrawal	Balance
31-Dec					1,000.00
1-Jan	1001	Rent		800.00	200.00
1-Jan	1002	Groceries		66.00	134.00
2-Jan	1003	Telephone		78.76	55.24
2-Jan		Contract 1	900.00		955.24
3-Jan	1004	Car payment		259.00	696.24
4-Jan	1005	Groceries		98.75	597.49
5-Jan	1006	Car Ins.		125.45	472.04
5-Jan	1007	Macy's		88.66	383.38
6-Jan	1008	Movies		24.75	358.63
7-Jan	1009	Utilities		86.44	272.19
8-Jan	1010	Groceries		86.65	185.54
10-Jan	1011	Cash Withdrawal		80.00	105.54
11-Jan		Contract 2	600.00		705.54
13-Jan	1012	Health Ins.		186.13	519.41
14-Jan		Contract 1	900.00		1,419.41
15-Jan	1013	Taxes		300.00	1,119.41
16-Jan	1014	Groceries		112.55	1,019.41
18-Jan	1015	Savings		100.00	951.41
20-Jan	1016	DMV/ticket		68.00	883.41
22-Jan	1017	Books R'Us		35.76	847.65
24-Jan	1018	Groceries		76.85	770.80
25-Jan	1019	Macy's		112.35	658.45
26-Jan	1020	Movies		24.75	633.70
28-Jan	1021	Dinner		38.98	594.72
30-Jan		Contract 2	600.00		1,194.72
30-Jan	1022	Groceries		44.66	1,150.06
31-Jan	1023	Cash Withdrawal		40.00	1,110.06

Figure 5.4. Check Register for the Jamesons

Your Turn

Figure 5.5 shows a personal financial spreadsheet, a check register. Part of the spreadsheet has been completed by the computer but the items from February 8 to February 15 have not been added or subtracted from the balance. The balance after each entry can be found by adding any new deposit to the *balance* column and then subtracting the check from the total. This gives you the new balance. It is the same thing you should do to figure your checkbook balance each time you write a check. The good thing about doing it with the spreadsheet is that all you have to do is record the deposit in the correct column and record the check in the *withdrawal* column. The spreadsheet then figures the balance for you. When you use a financial management spreadsheet that includes check writing, all you do is write the check and the spreadsheet enters it in the register and does all of the calculations for you. The spreadsheet is truly a gift to the small businessperson.

For practice, in figure 5.5, calculate the balance for the checking account after each transaction and complete the spreadsheet by hand. Yes, if you want to, you can use a calculator.

	A	B	C	D	E	F
	Date	Check#	Item	Deposit	Withdrawal	Balance
1						
2	31-Jan					1,111
3	1-Feb	1024	Rent		900.00	210.60
4	2-Feb		Contract 1	900.00		1,110.60
5	3-Feb	1025	Groceries		112.00	998.60
6	4-Feb	1026	Telephone		68.79	929.81
7	5-Feb	1027	Utilities		89.15	840.66
8	6-Feb	1028	Cash Withdrawal		80.00	760.66
9	7-Feb		Contract 2	600.00		1,360.66
10	8-Feb	1029	Car payment		259.00	
11	9-Feb	1030	Car Insurance		125.00	
12	10-Feb	1031	Groceries		84.16	
13	11-Feb	1032	Mervyn's		56.78	
14	12-Feb	1033	Tickets/Basketball		65.00	
15	13-Feb	1034	Health Insurance		186.13	
16	14-Feb		Contract 1	900.00		
17	15-Feb	1035	Savings		100.00	

Figure 5.5. Your Check Register

Chapter 6

Information in a Block

Bar Graphs and Column Graphs

This chapter will show you how to read and understand bar and column graphs. You will learn about their various formats and their many uses. You will also be able to amaze your boss and your coworkers by constructing bar graphs yourself.

Where You Will Find Them

Every issue of the newspaper, every news and business magazine, and every business office will have bar graphs for you to read. Bar graphs compare items to each other by showing quantities in bars or columns of information.

Some types of information that could be displayed in a bar chart include:

- sales per salesperson for one week (compares employee productivity)
- sales per department per month (compare departments)
- accidents per department per month (compare departments)
- expenses per day
- earnings per day

Bar graphs are constructed on a rectangular background. The sides of the rectangle are the axes of the graph, and serve as the bases for the units of measure and the categories that are being measured. The vertical axis, or Y-axis, is usually the value or measurement (how many or how much) axis. The X-axis, or horizontal axis, is usually the category (who, what, or when) axis.

 When you see a bar or column graph, think: This shows how these different things relate (or compare) to each other.

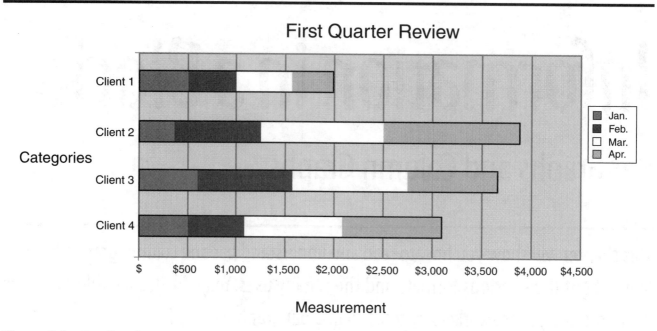

Figure 6-1a. Bar Graph

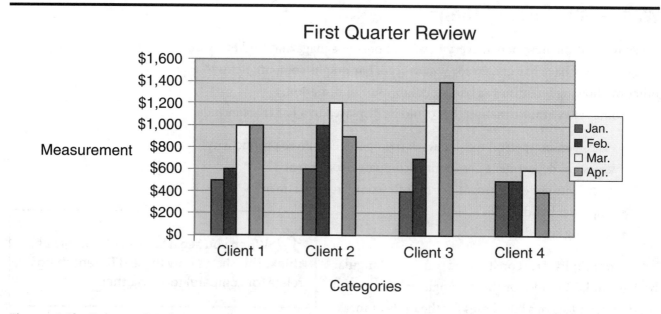

Figure 6.1b. Column Graph

Some reference books call both of these graphs "bar graphs" and some make a distinction between the two. They say that bar graphs show data in horizontal rectangles or bars and column graphs show data in vertical rectangles or columns.

When you are using a horizontal bar graph, the vertical axis is going to show the category and the horizontal axis will show the measurement. When you are using a column graph it is the opposite. Does it really make any difference? I don't think so. When you are making one of these graphs yourself, you can choose which display to use—horizontal or vertical—by deciding which display makes the clearest point. Remember, charts should make data more understandable, not more confusing.

If you want to show more than one quantity for a category, you will use a grouped bar graph. This is more than one bar or column for each category. You will see this often in magazines and newspapers.

Use the graphs in figure 6.2 (on the next page) to answer the following questions.

1. What is the main idea of the grouped column graph?

    _____

2. On the bar graph, what is the main idea of the graph?

    _____

3. Describe the main difference between the data on the two graphs.

    _____

4. Which sport has the same number of enrollees from each age group?
    a. basketball   b. swim team   c. football

5. Which sport has no one signed up for in the 5–6 year old group?
    a. tennis   b. ice hockey   c. gymnastics

6. Which sport has the highest total enrollment?
    a. soccer   b. softball   c. swim team

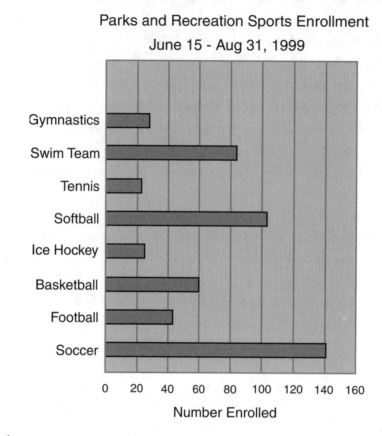

Figure 6.2a. Bar Graph

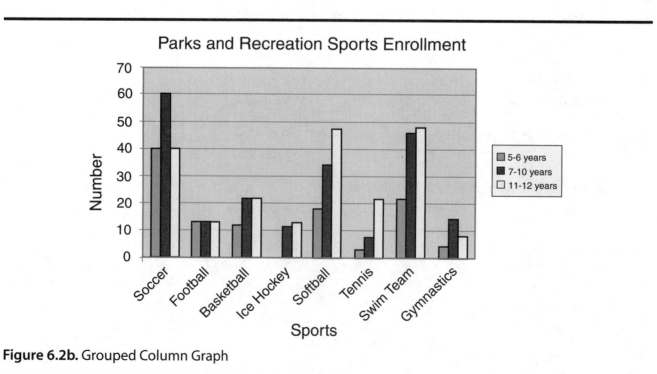

Figure 6.2b. Grouped Column Graph

Sales Results

Sometimes a graph shows a data series (several bits of data) for several categories, and multiple bars for each category will represent those. Figures 6.3a and 6.3b below are an example of this. Sometimes the data is stacked in a bar as in figure 6.3c. This graph shows total sales per day and each sales associate's contribution to the total sales.

Use the graphs in figure 6.3 to answer the following questions.

1. What is the main idea of figures 6.3a and 6.3b?
   a. They compare the daily sales of each sales associate for each day.
   b. They compare the percent of total sales for each associate by day.
   c. They compare the total sales for each day.

2. In 6.3a, which associate had the lowest total sales?
   a. Jessie   b. Thomas   c. Marie   d. Kate

3. In 6.3b, which associate had the highest sales for Sunday?
   a. Jessie   b. Kate   c. Marie   d. Thomas

4. In 6.3c, which associate sold the largest percent of total sales on Sunday?
   a. Jessie   b. Thomas   c. Marie   d. Kate

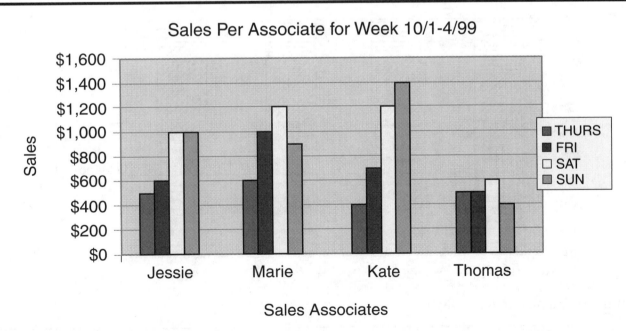

Figure 6.3a. Grouped Column Graph

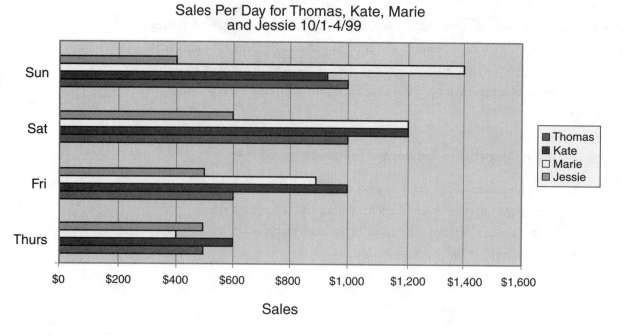

Figure 6.3b. Grouped Bar Graph

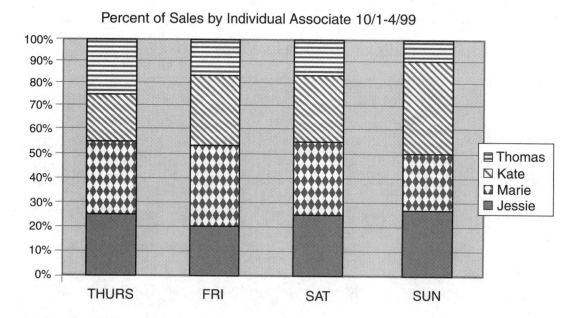

Figure 6.3c. Stacked Column Graph

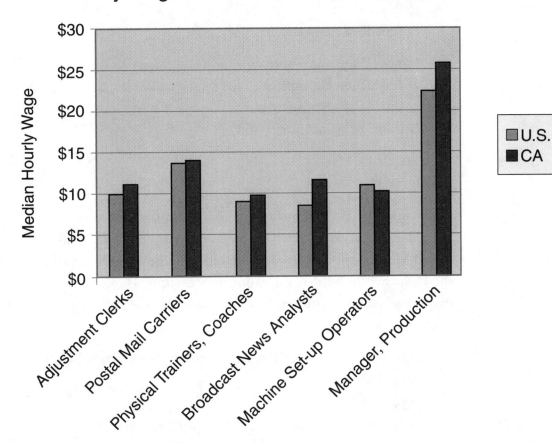

Figure 6.4. Hourly Wages for Selected Occupations

Comparing Hourly Wage Medians for Selected Occupations

Use the graph in figure 6.4 to answer the following questions.

1. What is the main idea of this graph?
    a. It compares the U.S. and California hourly wage median of six occupations.
    b. It shows the highest hourly wage median for the U.S. and California.
    c. It compares hourly wages of six different occupations with different education requirements.

2. Which occupation pays the highest hourly wage in California?
    a. Postal Mail Carriers
    b. Production Managers
    c. Broadcast News Analysts

3.   Which occupation pays the lowest hourly wage in California?
     a. Postal Mail Carriers
     b. Physical Trainers
     c. Broadcast News Analysts

4.   Which occupation requires the most education?
     a. Production Manager
     b. Broadcast News Analysts
     c. Information not given

Your Turn

Use the grid below to draw a bar graph using the following information:

Michael has decided to track his utility bills to see if he can lower his electricity bill. He has kept records for six months and he wants to create a bar graph to show whether the bills are increasing or decreasing. He also wants to identify the months when he consumes the most electricity and see if he can decrease his usage in those months.

1.   Record the following data on a chart for Michael by using the grid on the next page:

     1999
     January – $85.00   April – $88.00
     February – $75.00   May – $65.00
     March – $90.00   June – $96.00

2.   On the vertical axis, label even amounts of money. Five-dollar increments are suggested. Label this axis *Dollars*.

3.   On the horizontal axis, label six even bars and follow them up the vertical axis until they intersect. Label the axis *Months*.

4.   Color the bars.

Congratulations! You have just completed a bar graph that will help Michael analyze his utility bills. Now use that graph to answer the following questions.

1. Are Michael's bills increasing or decreasing?

    _____

2. In which month did he use the most electricity?

    _____

3. In which month did he use the least electricity?

    _____

Chapter 7

Information in a Line

Line Graphs

This chapter will show you how to read the "mountains" of information in line graphs. You will learn how to create them to show your own goals and your progress in meeting those goals.

Where You Will Find Them

Line graphs are used as often as bar graphs, so you will see them anywhere there is a need for a data display.

Your may think that a line graph looks like a range of mountains—or maybe one long, downhill ski run. (Or one long, downhill fall if you're not a skilled skier!) You'll be able relate to the "peaks and valleys" of a line graph as markers of progress toward your goals. You'll be able to see the direction of your progress at a single glance.

> ☀ **When you see a line graph, think:** Something is going up or down at different times or over a period of time.

Simple Line Graphs

A *simple line graph* shows one series of information, much like a simple bar graph. The vertical axis shows "how much" and the horizontal axis shows "what is being measured"—the categories, sequence, or quantity. These categories are labeled and one data point is right above each category on the horizontal axis.

Line graphs can be used for data that you want to track for highs, lows, and progress. You could use a line graph to track stock values, sales, defective products, errors, scores, exercise time, expenses, and many others. A simple line graph can track any one category of information.

Everett's Math Scores

Everett is in fifth grade and has been having trouble in math. He has decided to keep a graph of his monthly averages so he can see whether he is getting better or just staying in the same place. The figure below shows his line graph of these scores.

Use the graph in Figure 7.1 to answer the following questions.

1.   By how many points has Everett's math average improved by March?

   _____

2.   Which month's score is as low as September's?

   _____

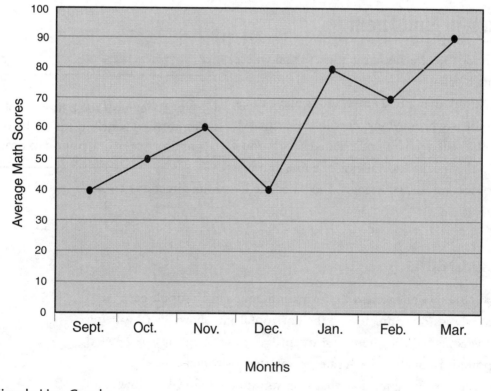

Figure 7.1. Simple Line Graph

3.   In which month were his scores next to highest?

_____

4.   Are Everett's scores getting higher or lower?

_____

Grouped Line Graphs

Grouped line graphs are useful for comparing scores or numbers for people, years, departments, or other entities. When several data series are shown on one line graph, each series is shown with a different line. For example, a grouped line graph could show daily sales for three sales associates.

You can see how this would look in Figure 7.2.

- The horizontal axis shows the days of the week.
- The vertical axis shows sales numbers.
- Each salesperson is represented by a different patterned line. These lines are explained in the legend.

Use the graph in Figure 7.2 to answer the following questions.

1.   Which sales associate had the lowest sales figures on Monday?
     a. Sol   b. Jeff   c. Maggie

Figure 7.2. Grouped Line Graph

2. Which sales associate had the highest sales figures on Monday?
    a. Sol
    b. Jeff
    c. Maggie

3. Which sales associate had the lowest sales figures for the week?
    a. Sol
    b. Jeff
    c. Maggie

4. Which sales associate had the highest sales figures for the week?
    a. Sol
    b. Jeff
    c. Maggie

5. On what day did all three sales associates have almost the same dollar amount in sales?
    a. Monday
    b. Friday
    c. Wednesday

Joyce's Exercise Graph

Joyce has decided she must incorporate more exercise into her daily routine. She used a line graph to record the actual time she spent exercising versus the goal she had set for herself. The graph below shows how her actual figures compared to her goal for a specific period of time (one week).

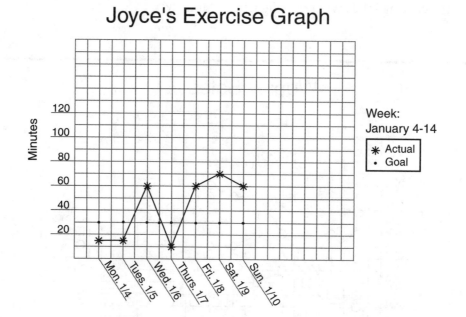

Figure 7.3. Grouped Line Graph

Use the graph in Figure 7.3 to answer the following questions.

1. How long did Joyce exercise on Saturday?
    a. 70 mins.   b. 65 mins.   c. 45 mins.

2. On which three days does Joyce exercise more than her minimum goal?
    a. Fri., Sat., Sun.   b. Sat., Sun., Mon.   c. Wed., Sat., Thurs.

3. On which days does Joyce miss her exercise goal?
    a. Tues., Fri., Sun.   b. Tues., Thurs., Mon.   c. Tues., Thurs., Sun.

4. How many more minutes does Joyce exercise on Saturday than she does on Thursday?

    _____

5. What is the average number of minutes per day that Joyce exercised this week?

    _____

Manufacturing Example

The grouped line graph in Figure 7.4 is an example of a line graph that you might find in a manufacturing plant. Instead of inspecting every tiny part, manufactur-

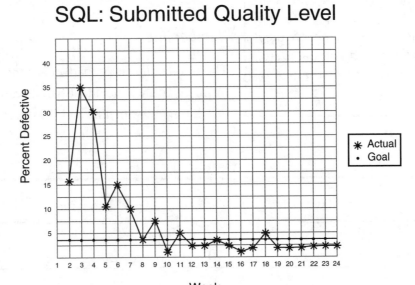

Figure 7.4. Percentage of Defective Parts

ers sometimes take a specific number of parts and inspect them. The number of defective parts in the submitted sample lets them figure the percentage of submitted quality level (SQL). This graph measures the percent of defective parts found in the SQL. All you need to know to interpret the chart is that the goal is to have a low percentage of defective SQL.

Use the graph in Figure 7.4 to answer the following questions.

1. During which week was the percentage of defective parts the greatest?
    a. 2   b. 3   c. 6

2. During which week did SQL first meet the goal SQL?
    a. 8   b. 18   c. 22

3. During which week did SQL reach 15%?
    a. 14   b. 6   c. 8

4. During which weeks was the SQL lower than the goal?
    a. 2, 4, 6   b. 16, 20, 24   c. 18, 20, 22

Mathematical Lines

Other types of line graphs are *mathematical lines*, which include the number line, the timeline, and the extent scale. These are all examples of graphics that show continuous movement along a single axis measured in numbers.

Number line

The *number line* is probably used more in school than in business, but we include it here because it is the basis for developing the timeline and the extent scale. The number

 **When you see a number line, think:** There's a line of numbers getting larger or smaller in equal amounts. If I go to the right, they get bigger. If I go to the left, they get smaller. If I go to the left and pass zero, they become negative, or less-than-zero, numbers.

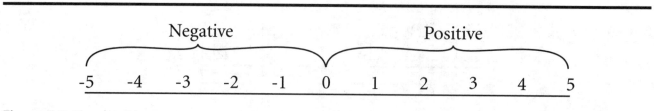

Figure 7.5. Number Line

line is a simple and useful graphic tool. Basically, it's a line with marks on it similar to a ruler. It was probably one of the first tools your teacher used to teach mathematics. A number line can also be called a *one-axis distribution graph* or *univariate graph*—now, aren't you glad we call it a number line?

Timeline

On a *timeline*, the measurement units progress in equal increments of time, such as months or years. Related events can be identified along this line. Sometimes it shows historical events, sometimes it displays more current occurrences such as orders placed, and sometimes it identifies tasks to be done in the future. Some timelines

> ☼ **When you see a timeline, think:** This shows when things happened over a period of time.

show categories of events in relationship to each other. For example, you could use a timeline to show two movements on one timescale, such as the development of classical music as compared to the historical art movement. Showing the two together allows the viewer to see how one movement may have affected the other. The timeline is the basis for developing the planning tool you will see in chapter 15, the Gantt chart.

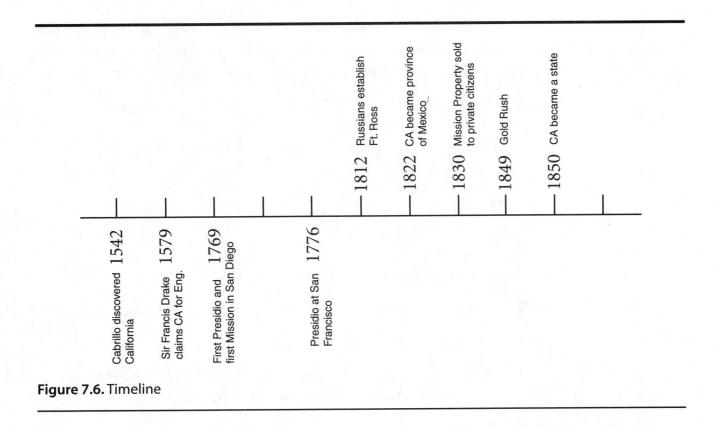

Figure 7.6. Timeline

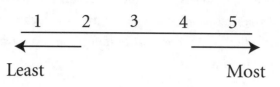

Figure 7.7. Extent Scale

| When you see an extent scale, think: This shows the how strongly a person feels about something or the degree to which it is happening. |

Extent Scale

An *extent scale* is a tool that allows the participant in a written survey to rank his/her opinion so that the survey-taker can have a numerical database to use for scoring. The participant gives his/her opinion an *extent rating*—how much do I agree or disagree, like it or dislike it—by circling a number.

Your Turn

Use the grid on the next page to draw a graph using the following information:

Jason has a new job as a retail salesperson. He works Wednesday through Sunday. His weekly sales goal is $3,000, or $600 per day for five days. Jason wants to keep track of his own sales and work to increase the amount of his weekly sales.

1. Plot the following information on a graph for Jason:
    Weekly goal: $600 per day
    Days worked: Wednesday, Thursday, Friday, Saturday, Sunday
    Actual sales per day:
    Wednesday – $400
    Thursday – $600
    Friday – $1,000
    Saturday – $1,200
    Sunday – $600

2. Label the vertical axis and mark the measurements in $200 increments.

3. On the horizontal axis label the sequence of days that Jason worked.

4. Record Jason's goal of $600 per day on each of the intersecting data points where the day meets the dollar amount. Connect the points.

5. Record Jason's actual sales in dollars for each day at the point where the day meets the dollar amount. There will be five points marked on the graph. Be

sure to use two different symbols to show his actual sales versus his target sales. You might use circles for actual sales and squares for target sales, for example.

6. Now connect the points.

7. Print a title on your graph.

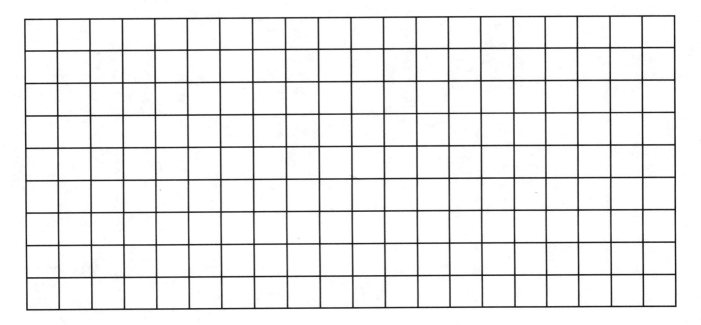

Terrific! You have just completed a line graph that will help Jason improve his sales performance. Now use that graph to answer the following questions.

1. Did Jason meet his weekly sales goal?

_____

2. Were his daily sales mostly above or below the daily goal?

_____

3. Which day is Jason's best sales day?

_____

Chapter 8

Shape Things Up with Histograms

In this chapter you will learn to recognize the message that is communicated by the shape of a histogram. In these graphics, two humps do not represent a camel and a bell doesn't symbolize music! When you see these shapes in a histogram, you will have an idea about how a process is going.

Where You Will Find Them

Histograms are similar to column graphs or bar graphs. They are used to study processes, production, and services for the purpose of improving them by finding patterns of occurrence. On these bar graphs, you get your first impression of the data from the pattern that the bars create. The histogram is the ideal tool for showing what shape you're in—or what shape your work process is in.

Histograms show information about the frequency of distribution of continuous data such as temperature, time, dimensions, weight, or speed. This information is useful for:

- putting customer information into measurable data
- studying a process
- displaying data in rank order
- clarifying the distribution of data

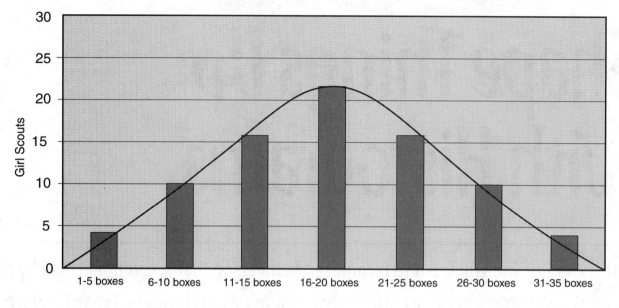

Figure 8.1. Distribution of Girl Scout Cookie Sales

-☼- **When you see a histogram shaped like a bell, think:** This is a group of measurements from a normal situation. These are no unexpected results here.

The vertical axis on a histogram shows frequency, or how many times each thing occurs. The horizontal axis shows the measurement value, or what is being counted.

Normal Distribution or Bell Curve

A good example of a *bell-shaped histogram* is how test scores for standardized tests are often analyzed in schools. On a single test, scores will probably fall into a normal distribution or bell curve when the test is taken under normal conditions. The normal distribution of scores will show a few scores that are very high, a few scores that are very low, and most of the scores in the middle. When you plot this data on a graph and draw a continuous line through the midpoints of the columns, you will get a histogram that looks a lot like a bell.

To create this histogram, you first collect data by using a tool similar to a check sheet. Next, organize the data from lowest points to highest points that fall

Achievement Test Scores

Total Test Score of 100% 88 participants

Score	Frequency	Total #
0-10%		0
11-20%	✓	1
21-30%	✓✓✓	4
31-40%	✓✓✓✓✓✓✓✓✓✓	13
41-50%	✓✓✓✓✓✓✓✓✓✓✓✓	15
51-60%	✓✓✓✓✓✓✓✓✓✓✓✓✓✓	17
61-70%	✓✓✓✓✓✓✓✓✓✓✓✓	15
71-80%	✓✓✓✓✓✓✓✓✓✓✓	13
81-90%	✓✓✓✓	4
91-100%	✓✓	2

Figure 8.2. Frequency Table of Achievement Test Scores

within the boundaries established for each bar. Record the data on a frequency table similar to the one below.

In figure 8.2 you can see that most of the scores were between 51% and 60%. The next two cells in frequency were the 41–50% range and the 61–70% range, and then the 31–40% range. Now you can show this same data on a histogram and it will clearly show a bell curve.

Use the graph in figure 8.3 to answer the following questions.

1. Which side of the histogram has the most scores in it?
   a. 0–60   b. 41–100   c. they are equal

2. Which of the following combinations of cells have the most scores in them?
   a. 0–20%   b. 11–30%   c. 71–90%

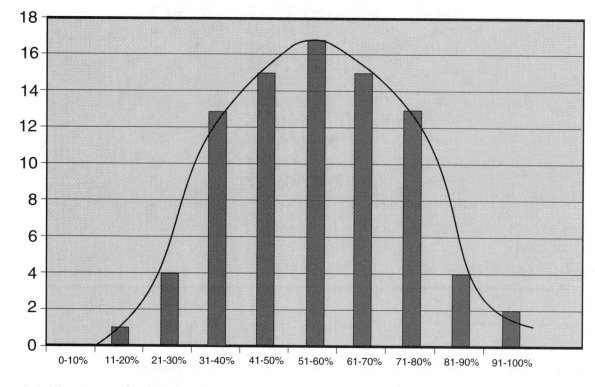

Figure 8.3. Histogram of Achievement Test Scores

Customer Service Calls

Seth works 12-hour shifts in customer support for a computer Internet provider. He currently handles 35–40 calls per day but his target number is 50 calls per day. He has a difficult time deciding how to increase his response yield, so he has decided to keep some frequency data.

Use the graph in figure 8.5 to answer the following questions.

1. Which side of the histogram has the most calls?
   a. 0–20 mins.   b. 16–30 mins.   c. they are equal

2. Does figure 8.5 show a normal distribution?

Length of Customer-Support Phone Calls Received

Length of call	Frequency	Total
0–5 mins.	✓✓	2
6–10 mins.	✓✓✓✓	5
11–15 mins.	✓✓✓✓✓✓	8
16–20 mins.	✓✓✓✓✓✓✓✓✓✓	14
21–25 mins.	✓✓✓	4
26–30 mins	✓✓✓	3
Over 30 mins.	✓✓	2
		38

Figure 8.4. Frequency Table of Customer Support Phone Calls

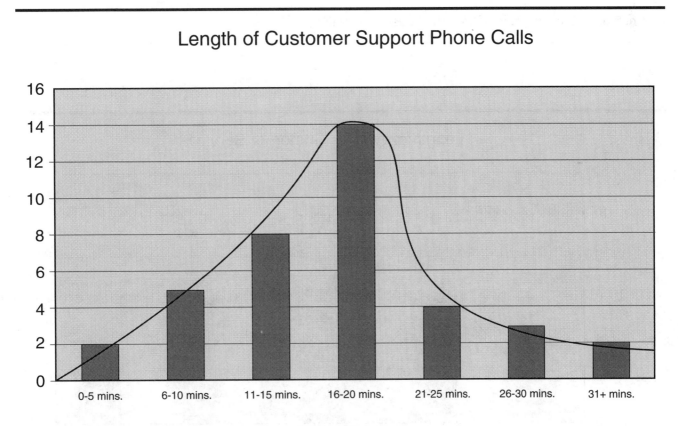

Figure 8.5. Histogram of Customer Support Phone Calls

The Customer's View

Seth's employer also wants to gather data on how long each customer has to wait on the telephone before they reach a customer service representative. In order to get this information, the wait times were automatically recorded for one day.

Length of Wait for Customer Service Representative

Length of wait	Frequency	Total
0-5 minutes	✓✓	2
6-11 minutes	✓✓✓✓✓	6
12-17 minutes	✓✓✓✓✓✓✓✓	10
18-23 minutes	✓✓✓✓✓	6
24-29 minutes	✓✓	2

Figure 8.6. Frequency Table of Length of Customer Wait

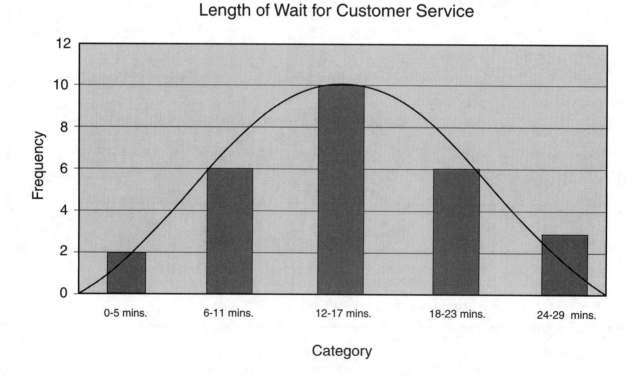

Figure 8.7. Histogram of Length of Customer Wait

Use the graph in figure 8.7 to answer the following questions.

1. If Seth's company has the goal of not letting customers wait for more than 15 minutes, is the information in figure 8.7 a normal distribution for length of telephone calls?

    a. yes   b. no

2. If Seth wants to decrease the waits that are longer than 15 minutes, he probably will have to:

    a. increase the time for some in the 6–11 group

    b. decrease the time in the 12–17 group

    c. both *a* and *b*

Other Shapes to Look For

The bell-shaped histogram represents a process that is behaving normally. The other shapes to identify are the *bi-modal*, the *cliff-like*, the *saw-toothed*, and the *skewed* histograms. Each of these shapes can communicate important information if you know how to recognize them.

Bi-modal

The bi-modal histogram has two separate high points—twin peaks. This means that the data was produced by more than one process. For example, it could be data from two machines, or material from two vendors.

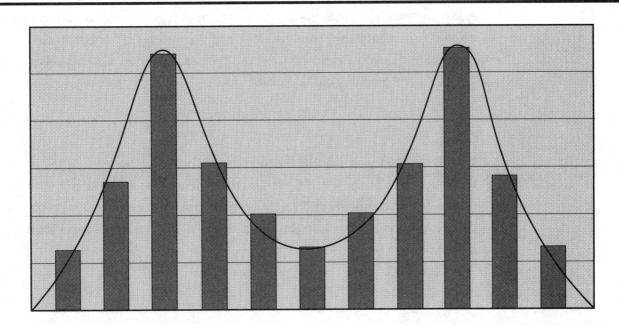

Figure 8.8. Bi-modal Histogram

Cliff-like

A cliff-like shape, appearing to end on a high measurement with no low point next to it, could mean that inspection or sorting has taken place to eliminate parts above or below a certain measurement.

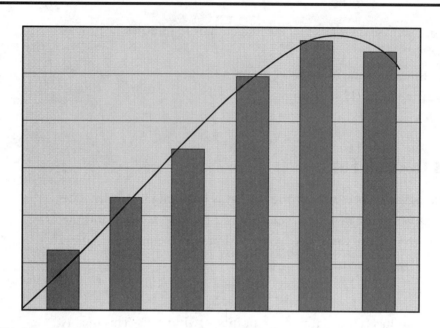

Figure 8.9. Cliff-like Histogram

Saw-toothed

A saw-toothed histogram has a jagged pattern of high and low bars. It may indicate measurement equipment problems such as poorly calibrated tools. The first impression that you should get from this type of histogram is *something is wrong*. The process is probably out of control.

Skewed

The skewed histogram shows the high measurement or the peak of the data too far to the right or the left. The ends are not mirrors of each other and the data peak is not in the middle as it would be in a normal distribution. This could mean that the process is functioning at a level that is too high (right-skewed) or too low (left-skewed).

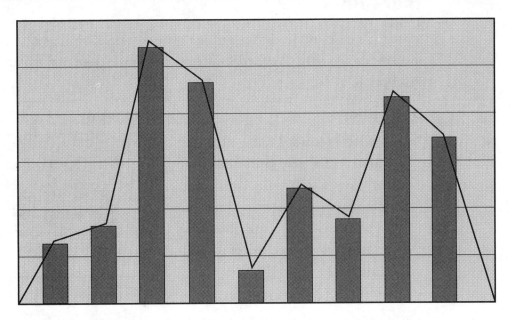

Figure 8.10. Saw-toothed Histogram

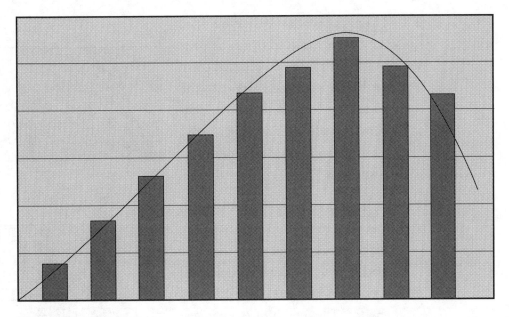

Figure 8.11. Skewed Histogram

Your Turn

Match the descriptions at the left with the information illustrated by the histograms on the right. Write the number of the histogram in the blank under the description.

Descriptions   **Histograms**

1. You have recorded salt content for samples of a new sauce that your company is mixing and packing. Samples were taken every hour for eight hours. The data show the process is completely out of control.
   Histogram _____

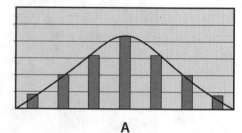

A

2. The samples that you have measured show a normal distribution of variation in salt. Your packaging process is in control.
   Histogram _____

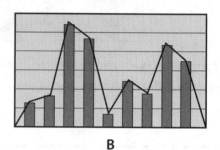

B

3. The pouches of sauce that were too salty were removed from the processing belt by an employee before the belt carried the product to the packaging department. At that point, Quality Control gathered information for the histogram.
   Histogram _____

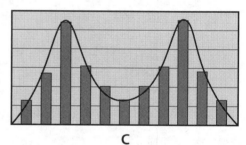

C

4. Material from two different vendors was used to produce widgets. The widgets were produced on the same machine but the change in material produced widgets of different lengths. The length of the widgets was sampled every hour for one day.
   Histogram _____

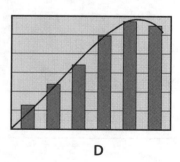

D

Congratulations! You are now a certified histogram interpreter (well, it is *almost* another language).

Chapter 9

The 80/20 Rule

Pareto Charts and Their Use in Problem Solving

In this chapter, you will learn about another useful business tool, the Pareto chart. It can help you figure out where to focus your best efforts. You will also learn to use some important business terms and concepts, which will help you stand out in the job market.

Where You Will Find Them

Just think how great it would be if you could focus your efforts on the 20% of the things in your life that get you the most results! You could spend your time doing the things that would help you reach your life goals the quickest. You could do the exercises that have the most impact on your health, cut the few foods out of your diet that account for most of your weight gain, study the topics that will account for most of your grade, and so on.

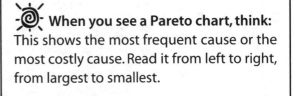 **When you see a Pareto chart, think:** This shows the most frequent cause or the most costly cause. Read it from left to right, from largest to smallest.

The Pareto chart is based on data that you collect and study to see if one issue is more significant than the others. It is a bar chart that displays categories of information from largest to smallest. This display clearly shows which category of information is the most frequent or the most costly.

The Pareto analysis lets you pinpoint what appears to be the category of data that is most important. It helps you separate the few vital causes from the many trivial causes. Many industries use the Pareto Chart and Pareto Analysis to find out the few important issues out of a group of issues to be solved, and then concentrate on those, since solving those few will get the greatest results.

The Pareto analysis and the Pareto chart were developed by Vilfredo Pareto (1848–1923), who studied the distribution of wealth in nineteenth-century Italy. With the data he gathered, he was able to prove that 80 percent of the wealth belonged to 20 percent of the population. Other statisticians proved this 80/20 rule to be true in many different studies and now it is a common business term. Sales departments often speak of the 80/20 rule, meaning 80% of sales come from 20% of the customers.

The bars on a Pareto chart never go up and down like a bell. They always go from high to low, like a ski slope.

Use the chart in figure 9.1 to answer the following questions.

1.   What is the type of data that is displayed in this chart?
      a. cost of living   b. family financial   c. business account

2.   Which two categories equal the same percent of the expenses?
      a. food and car
      b. entertainment and telephone
      c. entertainment and utilities

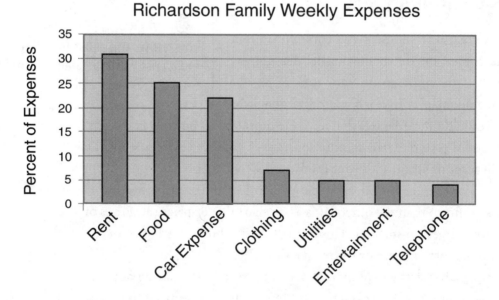

Figure 9.1. Richardson Family Weekly Expenses

3. Which two categories are the largest expenses?
    a. rent and food   b. entertainment and telephone   c. rent and car

4. Which category should we first look at closely in order to reduce the expenditures?
    a. rent   b. entertainment   c.   utilities

    Explain your answer to #4:

    _____

Who is the Best Customer?

Tim is a self-employed sign maker for local construction companies. His business is doing well and he is either going to have to get some more help or let some jobs go. He has decided to analyze his business with a Pareto chart to identify his best customers.

Use the chart in figure 9.2 to answer the following questions.

1. Which customer contributed most of Tim's revenue?
    a. Big Shot Builders   b. FixIt Quick Inc.   c.   UNamIt Inc.

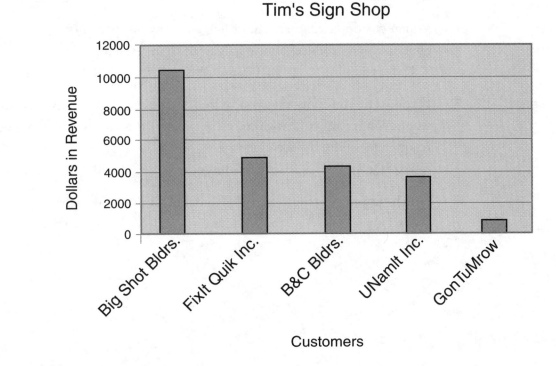

Figure 9.2. Tim's Sign Shop Revenues

2. Which customer appears to be the least productive for Tim?
    a. FixIt Quick Inc.   b. B&C Builders   c. GoneTuMrow

After analyzing revenue contributions, Tim decided to look at the amount of work it took to service each customer. He billed his sign construction service by the hour for his own work. However, he remembered his office assistant Maggie talking about extra paperwork for some customers. If that were the case, it would affect his decision. So, Maggie gave him the hourly breakdown for each client. He constructed another Pareto chart for this analysis.

Use Tim's Pareto charts in figures 9.2 and 9.3 to answer the following questions.

1. In figure 9.3, it is better for the customer to have:
    a. highest hours   b. lowest hours   c. middle hours

2. Which of Tim's customers takes the most office work to produce the revenue results?
    a. GonTuMrow   b. Big Shot Builders   c. FixIt Quik Inc.

3. Big Shot Builders requires how many hours of office work to produce $10,500 in revenue?
    a. 52 hours   b. 24 hours   c. 48 hours

4. Which customer requires about half as many hours of office work as Big Shot does and produces almost half as much in revenue?
    a. FixIt Quik   b. UNamit Inc.   c. B&C Builders

5. If you were Tim, now that you've looked at both charts, which customer would you try to work with in order to lower the number of office hours required to service the accounts?
    a. FixIt Quik   b. UNamit Inc.   c. B&C Builders

6. Which customer seems to have the potential for more business?
    a. FixIt Quik   b. UNamit Inc.   c. GonToMrow

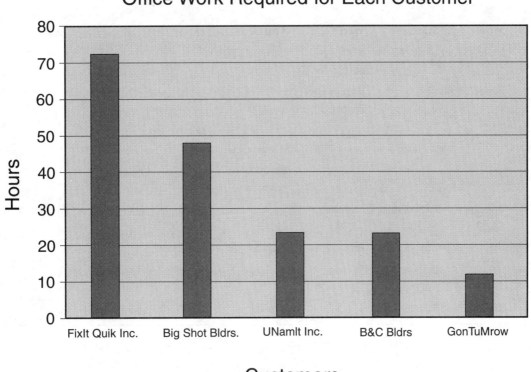

Figure 9.3. Office Work Required for Each Customer

Your Turn

You may wonder how keeping a record and analyzing data can help you in your everyday life. One way to figure that out is to look at this story about Kim Roberts.

The Roberts family has three teenagers, who each receive $60.00 per week for their allowance. Two of the teenagers, Rick and Julie, make their money last for an entire week but Kim, the third teenager, always comes up short before the end of the week. In an effort to help the teenagers budget their money better, the Roberts give each of them a log in which they can enter their expenditures for the next week. The teenagers will use this information to study what they actually spend and determine where they would like to make changes in their spending habits.

Kim is sure that she only spends what she needs to and that she can't cut back. Like her brother and sister, she faithfully keeps a record of her main expenditures for one week using the following log:

WEEKLY EXPENSE LOG

Name: Kim Roberts   Week _____

	Mon	Tues	Wed	Thurs	Fri	Sat	Sun	TOTAL
Breakfast	Latte -$2.40	Latte- $2.40	Muffin/ coffee-$3.50	Latte- $2.40				$10.70
School Supplies	Paper-$3.00		Binder for report-$2.95					$5.95
Personal Care					Hairspray- $7.95			$7.95
Clothing				Layaway payment-$10				$10.00
Lunch	Lunch- $4.60	Jamba Juice- $4.50	Lunch- $3.79	Lunch- $2.45	Lunch- $2.65		Yogurt-$2.40 soda-$1.25	$21.64
Transportation	Bus -$1.30	Bus -$1.30	Bus -$1.30	Bus -$1.30	Bus -$1.30			$6.50
Entertainment		Fashion Mag -$3.95			Movie- $4.50	Dance- $5.00		$13.45
TOTAL	$11.30	$12.15	$11.34	$16.15	$16.46	$5.00	$3.65	$76.05

1. How much did Kim spend over her allowance?

   She spent: _____

   Her allowance: _____

   Amount she spent over her allowance: _____

2. Using the information in Kim's log, select the category on which she spent the most money and write the category and the amount in space *a* below. List the other categories in descending order of amount in the additional spaces. Round off each amount to the nearest dollar. (If the cents amount to $.50 or over, round to the dollar above; if the cents amount to $.49 and under, round to the dollar below.)

   a. _____

   b. _____

   c. _____

   d. _____

   e. _____

   f. _____

   g. _____

3.   Using the rectangle below:
*   Use the vertical axis to show amounts of money spent. Divide this axis into even increments. Draw "tick" marks to show even amounts of money and label this axis **Dollars**.
*   Label the horizontal axis **Expenses**.
*   Mark seven even spaces on the horizontal axis (the bottom line) that will represent the categories.
*   Arrange and write these category labels from largest to smallest, with the largest at the left bottom corner of the rectangle.
*   Draw bars for each category that match the amount shown on the vertical axis.
*   Color each bar or create a pattern for each.

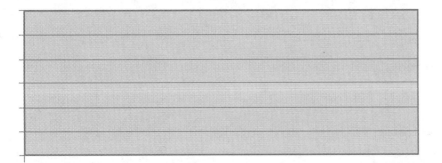

Great job! You have not only analyzed the information in Kim's expense log, but also used it to create a Pareto chart. Now use that chart to answer the following questions.

1.   In which category could Kim decrease expenses easily?

_____

2.   How could she use the log and the Pareto analysis to monitor her spending?

_____

_____

Chapter 10

Stay within the Lines

Run Charts and Control Charts

In this chapter you will learn to recognize and interpret run charts and control charts. These are useful to companies as they try to improve their products and service to customers. Run charts and control charts signal quality problems before they become huge. Knowing what these charts are used for and how to read them is a skill that will put you out in front in the race for jobs.

Where You Will Find Them

Run charts and *control charts* are line graphs that have the special purpose of keeping track of product quality and controlling a process. Run charts show a record of data over a sequential period of time. Control charts indicate what happened in the past when the process was running well and it plots current data on that guide. All types of manufacturing companies use these charts to monitor their processes, and now other industries are catching on to them as well. Companies that use them include food processing companies that prepare sauces and other foods, companies that make plastic parts, companies that make metal parts, and companies that put liquids into containers.

Many of these charts are printed by computers, which monitor the production machinery. Workers are expected to understand the main idea of the charts and how to read them.

Run Charts

Run charts are line graphs that show actual sequential measurements of a process over a period of time. Since measurements are taken at regular intervals, the run chart can show trends in a repetitive process or task. For example, the degree of doneness of cookies could be measured for each batch of cookies. You would begin to see if you are burning more cookies each time or if they are under-cooked. Is there a trend? Or you could measure the amount of juice you get from 10 lemons. Are you getting a similar amount each time or is there a large variation in amount? How about servings of yogurt? Are the servings the same size each time or does the size vary from serving to serving?

> ☀ **When you see a run chart, think:**
> This shows sequential measurements of a repetitive process over a period of time.

The horizontal axis on a run chart is almost always the sequence or time axis. The vertical axis almost always shows measurement. These charts are used to detect quality problems so that they can be eliminated.

Run charts usually show specific limits as set by the customer, the government, or the manufacturer. The limits are shown on the chart and the measurements, or actual data points, are plotted on the same chart.

Cookie Yield per Batch of Dough

Joyce works as a baker in the Mill Valley Sweet Shop. She wants to get the same number of cookies out of each batch of mix. She has decided to monitor the yield of each batch to see how similar the individual yields are to each other.

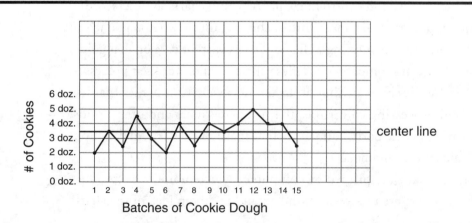

Figure 10.1. Cookie Dough Yield

Use the run chart in figure 10.1 to answer the following questions.

1. Which batch of cookies had the highest yield?
   a. batch 13   b. batch 12   c. batch 4

2. Which batch of cookies had the lowest yield?
   a. batch 15   b. batch 3   c. batch 1

3. What quantity did the largest number of batches yield?
   a. 4 dozen plus   b. 2 dozen   c. 3 dozen

Patient Wait Time

Dr. Jennings has a policy that no patient should wait more than a half hour to see a doctor in his health maintenance facility. He has heard complaints from some patients that they have been in the waiting room for an hour or more. His staff says that is not true, so he has kept a run chart to record the actual wait times.

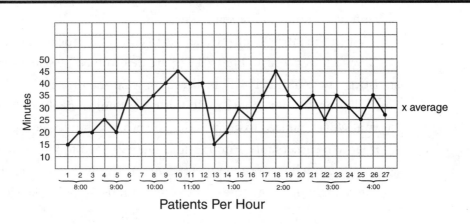

Figure 10.2. Dr. Jennings' Patients' Waiting

Use the run chart in figure 10.2 to answer the following questions.

1. At what time of day do patients wait for 30 minutes or less?
   a. 8:00 a.m. and 1:00 p.m.
   b. 3:00 p.m. and 4:00 p.m.
   c. 11:00 a.m. and 2:00 p.m.

2. At what time of day do patients wait the longest?
   a. 8:00 a.m. and 1:00 p.m.
   b. 11:00 a.m. and 2:00 p.m.
   c. 3:00 p.m. and 4:00 p.m.

3.   Does this chart show any patient waiting over 1 hour?

    a. yes   b. no

Control Charts

Control charts are similar to run charts but they are used primarily for keeping a process in control. They are usually based on what has happened in the past. Occasionally, they are based on a run chart.

 **When you see a control chart, think:** This measures whether a process, over time, is taking place within acceptable limits.

The information plotted on control charts is usually averages of actual data. That means that each data point shows the average of several samples of data. For example, if you want to keep the weight of individual cookies the same and you use five cookies for each sample of the product, the point that is plotted would be the average weight of the five cookies. To get this you would weigh each cookie, add up all the weights, and divide the answer by 5. You would plot this weight on your chart, and then at regular intervals you would repeat the process.

When the purpose of the chart is to control a process, upper control limits (UCL) and lower control limits (LCL) are determined by using some very precise statistics. These numbers will be based on what the process has done in the past. You will probably never have to do this because most likely a computer will do it for you. What you need to know is that the process should stay between those lines in order to be acceptable. Another line you will need to know about is the "average" line, central line, or center line (CL or $\overline{\overline{x}}$). This is the average of all of the averages, and it falls in the middle of the control limits. It looks like Figure 10.4.

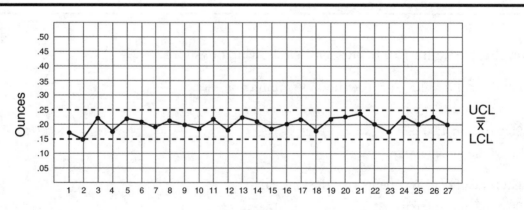

Figure 10.3. Cookie Weights

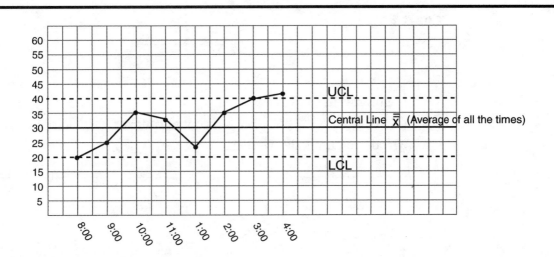

Figure 10.4. Center Line

The other term you need to know for understanding control charts is the term "range." Control charts that show ranges are called *R charts*. Range is the difference between the lowest amount and the highest amount in a subgroup or sample. If a batch of Joyce's cookies varied in weight from .01 ounces to .25 ounces, the range would be .24 ounces. You could have 12 people in a class with an age range from 20 years of age to 35 years of age, or a range of 15 years. When high quantities of product are being produced, several samples may be taken from each production run.When that is the case, plotting the ranges for that sample gives us useful information. A process that is in trouble shows up faster when ranges are recorded.

Dr. Jennings' HMO Waiting Room

We learned in an earlier example that Dr. Jennings does not want anyone waiting more than 30 minutes to see a doctor. By keeping a record of wait times, we verified that patients did often have to wait more than 30 minutes. Corrections were made in procedures and more attention is now being paid to improving the wait time. Hours where the longest waits were recorded are now staffed with more personnel in order to reduce wait time. Figure 10.5 shows the current wait time information by averaging the wait time for all patients who sign in between specific times.

Figure 10.5. Dr. Jennings' HMO

Use the control chart in figure 10.5 to answer the following questions.

1. According to figure 10.5, is the HMO's wait time now within control limits?
    a. yes   b. no

2. Which two hours are still at risk for longer waits?

    _____

What to Look For

When a process is in control, you will see the following signs when you look at the control chart:

1. Most of the points will be in the middle one-third of the area between the control limits.
2. All points will be inside the UCL and the LCL.
3. Points will occur in no specific pattern.

When a process is out of control, you will see these signs:

1. At least one point outside, or directly on, one of the control limits.
2. Seven consecutive points moving in the same direction, either up or down, indicating a change in the process.
3. Changes in the random pattern of points, which means that something has changed in the process.

Practice interpreting control charts using the following charts. You don't have to know statistics—you don't have to even know what the process is that is being monitored. You can just interpret the control charts.

Chart 1

1. The process in chart 1 is:
    a. in control   b. going out of control
    Why do you think this is true?

    _____

Chart 2

2.   The process in chart 2 is:
     a. in control   b. going out of control
     Why do you think this is true?

_____

Chart 3

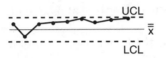

3.   The process in chart 3 is:
     a. in control   b. going out of control
     Why do you think this is true?

_____

Chart 4

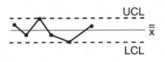

4.   The process in chart 4 is:
     a. in control   b. going out of control
     Why do you think this is true?

_____

Your Turn

Use the following information to create a control chart:

Bill and Maggie are the founders of Bag O' Bites Candy, a company that makes and packages homemade candies for sale. They know that they must put approximately the same amount of candy in each package in order to please their customers and also make a profit.

They use a candy scoop to pick up and deposit the candy in each sack. They try to fill the scoop with an equal amount each time. However, their customers have been saying that the bags do not always contain the same amount. In addition, Bill and Maggie are having a hard time making a profit, so they don't want to waste any candy. The upper limit of bags in the past has been 43 pieces of candy and the lower limit has been 35 pieces. The average number of pieces is 39. They decide to monitor the bag-filling operation by taking sample bags every hour and counting the candies. So every hour they take three bags, count the number of candies, average the amount, and then plot it on the graph. You can get some experience creating a control chart if you help them out.

1. Label the time intervals on the horizontal axis. (8:00, 9:00, 10:00, 11:00, etc.)

2. Label the measurement axis in increments of 5. (5, 10, 15, pieces of candy)

3. Draw a broken line for the upper control limit at 43. Label it UCL.

4. Draw a solid line for the center line at 39. Label it CL.

5. Draw a broken line for the lower control limit at 35. Label it LCL.

6. Average the sample bags and put the point on the chart.
    Example: For 8:00 a.m. samples, add 36+40+42 and divide the answer by 3 to get the average.

8:00 a.m. — 36, 40, 42	12:00 p.m. — 35, 38, 37
9:00 a.m. — 41, 37, 40	1:00 p.m. — 39, 36, 38
10:00 a.m. — 39, 42, 37	2:00 p.m. — 38, 41, 39
11:00 a.m. — 40, 38, 41	3:00 p.m. — 42, 40, 43

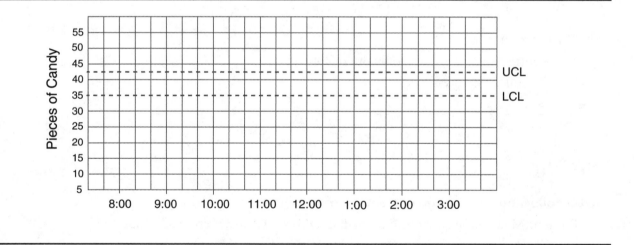

Great job! You have created a control chart for Bill and Maggie's Bag O' Bites Candy, and helped them to monitor their business.

Chapter 11

It Matters How You Slice It

Pie Charts

This chapter will show you how to read and create pie charts. Pie charts offer a clear and easy way to organize data. They can be very impressive when you add color to the different "slices" of the pie.

Where You Will Find Them

Pie charts can be found everywhere. They are as common as weather maps and financial charts. They are not only easy to read and fun to make, but also easy to understand. Think of the last time you saw a pie or a pizza divided among several people. Remember how easy it was to figure out who got the biggest piece or who ate the most pieces? A pie chart makes information just that easy to understand and remember.

> ☀ **When you see a pie chart, think:**
> Who, or what, gets the biggest piece of the whole pie? Who gets the other pieces?

The idea of a pie divided into several pieces is used to introduce fractions in school because it is a good tool for showing that segments of a whole thing equal a percent of the whole.

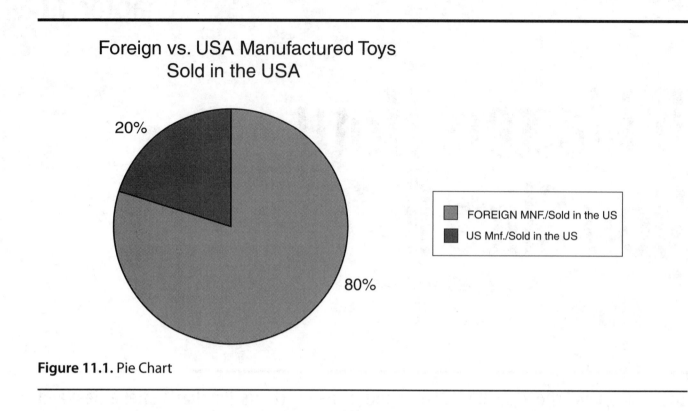

Figure 11.1. Pie Chart

The unique quality of the pie chart is the fact that it shows you the overall picture of the data as well as a picture of the individual pieces of data. You can immediately see where the pizza went and whether or not there is any left. Another characteristic is that the percent of the whole is printed right on the pie segment. There are no measurements to figure out; no hatch marks to read. The measurements are all displayed for you on the pie chart.

Where Did the Pizza Go?

Use the chart in figure 11.2 to answer the following questions.

1. Which team member ate as much as two other players?
    a. Jane   b. Tommy   c. Carl

2. The coach ate how many times as much pizza as Edie ate?
    a. 2   b. 3   c. 4

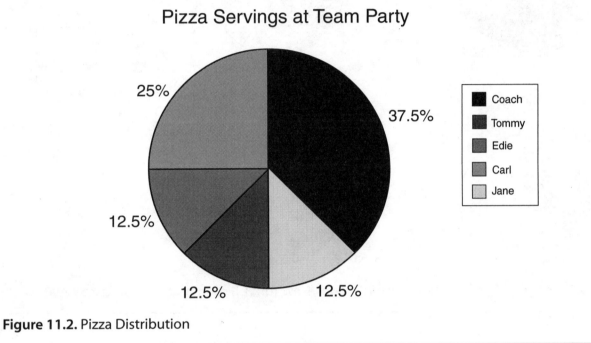

Figure 11.2. Pizza Distribution

High Hopes Media Group, Inc.

The High Hopes Media Group, Inc., wants to invest money in a cable TV network company in one of the major metropolitan areas. This investment would target the fastest growing ethnic population in the selected city. They have gathered information about Los Angeles, New York, Chicago, and San Francisco, which is displayed in the pie charts below.

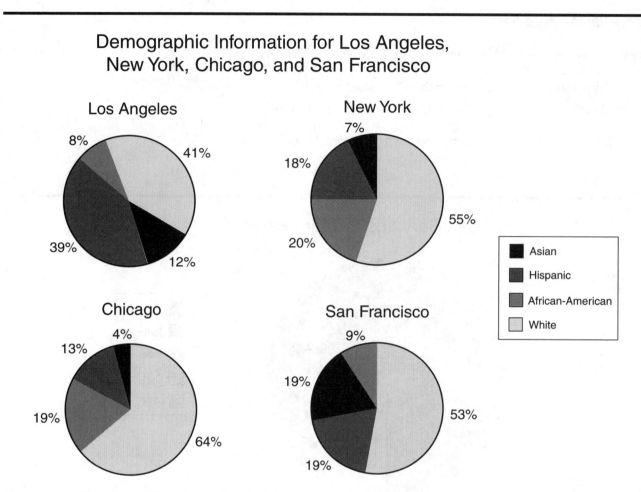

Figure 11.3. Demographic Information for Los Angeles, New York, Chicago, and San Francisco Areas

Use the charts in figure 11.3 to answer the following questions.

1. In figure 11.3 you are given ethnic demographic information for four major cities—Los Angeles, New York, Chicago, and San Francisco. Which city would best support a Hispanic language television station?
    a. Los Angeles   b. New York   c. Chicago   d. San Francisco

2. Which city would support more investment in an Asian television station?
    a. Los Angeles   b. New York   c. Chicago   d. San Francisco

3. Which city has the smallest percent of white population?
    a. Los Angeles   b. New York   c. Chicago   d. San Francisco

4. Which city has the smallest Asian population?
    a. Los Angeles   b. New York   c. Chicago   d. San Francisco

Iman Independent Contractor

Teresa started her own office cleaning service this year. She now has six clients and works as a subcontractor. One company, the Lucky Strike Association, contracted her services two months later than the other five. She now has so many jobs that she either has to hire more employees or drop one client. If she decides to drop a client, it needs to be the one that makes her the least money. The following pie chart shows the total amounts of business each company does with Teresa.

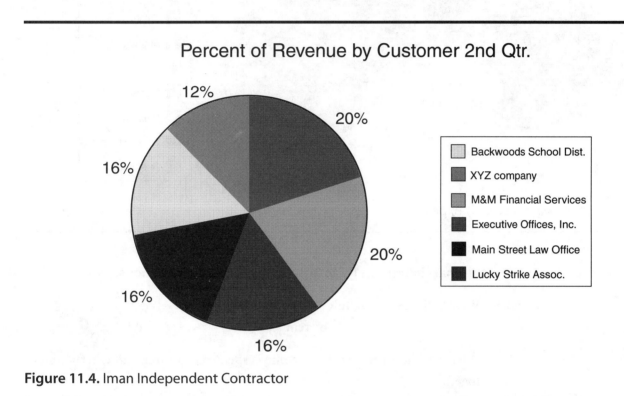

Figure 11.4. Iman Independent Contractor

Use the chart in figure 11.4 to answer the following questions.

1. Which company should Teresa drop?
   a. Backwoods School District
   b. XYZ Company
   c. M&M Financial

2. Which companies are her biggest clients?
   a. Lucky Strike and Executive Offices
   b. Backwoods School District and M&M Financial
   c. Executive Offices and M&M Financial

Edison Family Expenses

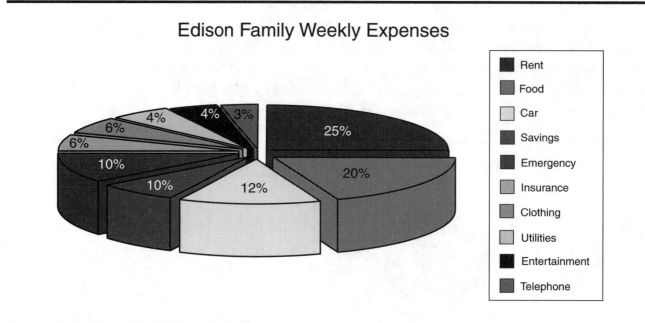

Figure 11.5. Edison Family Weekly Expenses

Use the chart in figure 11.5 to answer the following questions.

1. What is the Edison family's biggest weekly expense?

   a. car   b. rent   c. food

2. What percent of the weekly income is spent on clothing and entertainment together?

   _____

3. Food is 20% of the weekly expense and the total expense is $500. How much does the Edison family spend on food?

   _____

4. Which three expense categories account for just over half of the weekly expenses?

   a. rent, food, car   b. rent, food, telephone   c. rent, food, utilities

Demographics for Small City Planning

The City Council of Watchusgro, Arizona is creating a development plan for the town, and is trying to predict future needs for housing, schools, shopping, and entertainment centers. Right now, there is very little shopping in Watchusgro, and no entertainment industry outside of school and church activities. The City Council is using the most recent census numbers, which are displayed on the following pie chart.

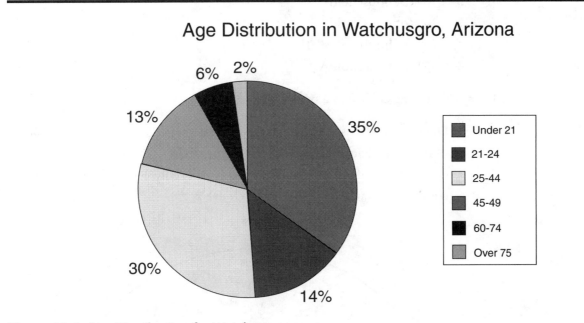

Figure 11.6. Age Distribution for Watchusgro

Use the chart in figure 11.6 to answer the following questions.

1. What is the largest age group in this small town?
   a. Under 21   b. 45–59   c. 25–44

2. What percent of the population is under the age of 45?
   a. 65%   b. 79%   c. 30%

3. According to the information in figure 11.6, which of the following facilities should the City build?
   a. skating rink/party facility   c. a Sesame Street Amusement Center
   b. a Senior Citizen Center   d. a theater complex with restaurants

   Why? _____

   _____

Your Turn

Make a pie chart to show the following information:

An independent company surveyed the households in a condominium housing development called Cementblock City. They gathered the following information:

Number of children per household:

4+ 5% of households

3   10% of households

2   20% of households

1   20% of households

0   45% of households

Use the following circle and a pencil.

- Draw a line across the circle at the halfway mark. You now have two halves of the circle. Each half equals 50% of the circle.
- On the top half, draw a line that divides it evenly. Each of these two parts equals one quarter, or 25%, of the circle.

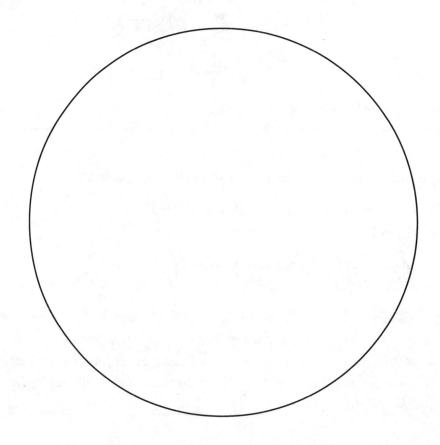

- If the 25% is divided equally into five parts, each part is equal to 5% of the circle. On the first quarter of the circle, draw a line that shows one 5% piece.
- Move down to the largest piece of the circle, the 50% piece. Draw a line that shows another 5% piece. Make sure that this 5% piece is next to the one in the quarter above.
- Since you know that the half of the circle equals 50%, marking off a 5% piece means that the remaining piece equals 45%. This 45% piece represents your largest bit of information.
- You should now have two 5% pieces next to each other. Join these two together by coloring or shading for a 10% piece. The remaining large piece of the first quarter is equal to 20% of the circle.
- Now move to the second quarter of the circle. Draw a line that shows one 5% piece. The remaining large piece of the second quarter is equal to 20% of the circle.

Great job so far! Your pie chart should have one piece for each of the five categories of information:

4+	**5%** of households
3	**10%** of households
2	**20%** of households
1	**20%** of households
0	**45%** of households

- Now you want to label each category. You can just label the data right on the chart or you can make a legend. If you want to, you can color each piece a different color and then use the colors in the legend.
- Give your graph a title.
- Show it off!

Chapter 12

X Marks the Spot

Point Graphs and Scattergrams

Seeing spots before your eyes? Don't worry—this chapter will show you how to interpret them! You will learn what it means when spots in a graph are grouped in a long line and what it means when they are scattered randomly.

Where You Will Find Them

Point graphs are a family of graphs that show quantitative information as data points represented by dots, squares, triangles, or other symbols. Graphs in this family have several different names: *point graph*, *scatter graph*, *scattergram*, *scatter plot*, and so on. These graphs all display quantitative measurement on the vertical axis. The factor that distinguishes one from another is the type of data displayed on the horizontal axis. If the horizontal axis displays categorical information (such as wood, steel,

> ☼ **When you see a point graph or scattergram, think:** Two things are related if the dots are "flying" together in a diagonal line from left to right.

aluminum, titanium), then the graph is a point graph. If the horizontal axis shows quantitative measurement, the graph is a scattergram or scatter graph.

Simple Point Graph

The simple point graph is used to display collected data about different categories. You might gather information about the movie attendance habits of the population in a specific location. The categories could be pre-teen, teenager, 18–30-year-

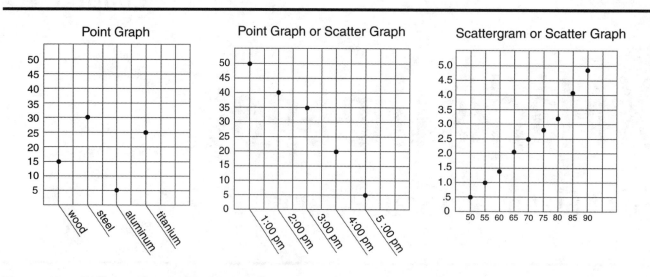

Figure 12.1. Different Types of Point Graphs

olds, 31–50-year-olds, and over 50. If you collect data about the number of movies attended last year, you could display that data on a point graph. No cause-and-effect relationship is indicated but important information about movie attendance of these age groups could be displayed effectively using a point graph.

Use the graph in figure 12.2 to answer the following questions.

1. Which age group or groups goes to the movies the most?

    _____

2. Which group goes to the movies the least?

    _____

3. According to the information on this graph, if a large number of teenagers are about to turn 18 and the 18–30-year-old group has only a few people turning 31, is the existing theater big enough?
    a. yes
    b. no
    c. There is not enough information given to answer this question.

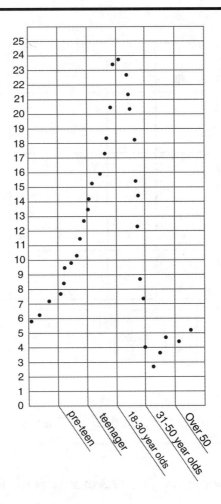

Figure 12.2. Movie Attendance in Pine Mountain

Point Graph of Solder Defects

The point graph shows quickly where the problems are. In the example shown in figure 12.3, each board has 655 opportunities for something to be wrong, either solder defects or misalignment or misplacement of one of the many components. There were more than 40 solder voids in one of the boards. There were no solder bridges. There were exactly 40 places where excess solder was found in one of the boards. One of the boards had insufficient solder in 12 places and another board had insufficient solder in almost 30 places. Each of the five boards had misaligned and misplaced parts. This is where most of the problems—the defects—are.

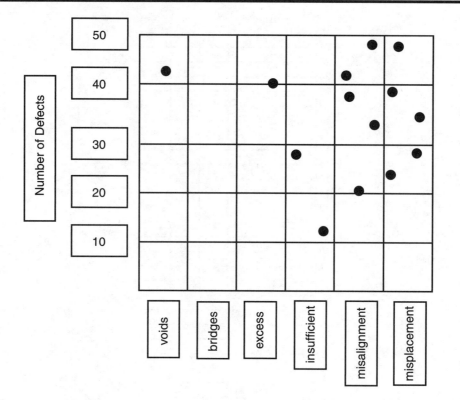

Figure 12.3. Point Graph of Solder Defects on Printed Circuit Boards

Use the graph in figure 12.3 to answer the following questions.

1.   In which two categories are most of the defects or errors on the boards?

_____

2.   Which category was not found at all?

_____

Scattergrams

Scattergrams are used to display and study the relationship between one *variable* (something that changes or has the ability to change) and another. They can show what happens to one process when another process changes. They are especially useful when you are looking for a cause-and-effect relationship.

Managers have long used these graphs, and now front-line employees use them too. It is to your advantage to know what they mean when you see them. To make one, you need to collect 50 to 100 paired samples, such as gas mileage and speed. Does one affect the other? Does yearly income affect frequency of movie attendance? In a particular area, does income affect private school enrollment in families with school-age children?

The variable you suspect to be the cause is measured on the horizontal axis and the variable you expect to be the effect is measured on the vertical axis. Both measurements will be quantitative. When the data are plotted on these axes, they will form patterns and the relationships will be easy to **spot**! (Sorry, I couldn't resist.)

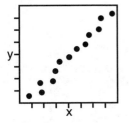

Positive Correlation

Dots cluster together tightly along an imaginary line from lower left corner to upper right corner. It looks like a kite tail with dots clustered around it.

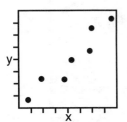

Weak Correlation

Dots cluster loosely along an imaginary line from lower left corner to upper right corner. Dots are loosely gathered with more space between them.

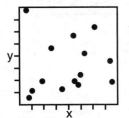

No Correlation

Dot clusters are all over the place with no distinct pattern. This indicates that there is no connection, either positive or negative, between the two variables.

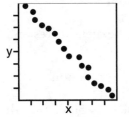

Negative Correlation

Dots cluster together tightly along an imaginary line from lower right corner to upper left corner. It looks like a kite tail with dots clustered around it, flying to the left. This pattern indicates a definite negative correlation.

Monthly Income and Food Expenditures

A group of social scientists wanted to investigate the relationship of food expenditures to income levels. They surveyed families to find out what they spent on food each month and the amount of their monthly income. The following scattergram plots the two variables. You can tell it's a scattergram because both variables can, and do, change.

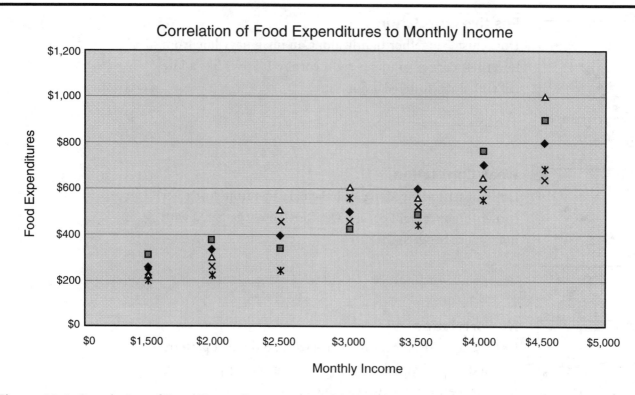

Figure 12.4. Correlation of Food Expenditures to Monthly Income

Use the graph in figure 12.4 to answer the following questions.

1. According to figure 12.4, the correlation between food expenditures and amount of income is

   a. negative   b. positive   c. no correlation

2. What is the least and the most that the family that makes $4,500 a month spends on food?

   a. $375 / $500   b. $500 / $600   c. $650 / $1,000

Manufacturing Errors and Hours of the Work Day

The Airsafe Bolt Company needed to reduce errors in their manufacturing process. A process improvement team began an investigation on the first shift. They suspected that errors increased as the workers became tired at the end of the day. To investigate, for ten days they counted the errors in their product during each hour after 12:00 p.m.

The results of this investigation are displayed in figure 12.5.

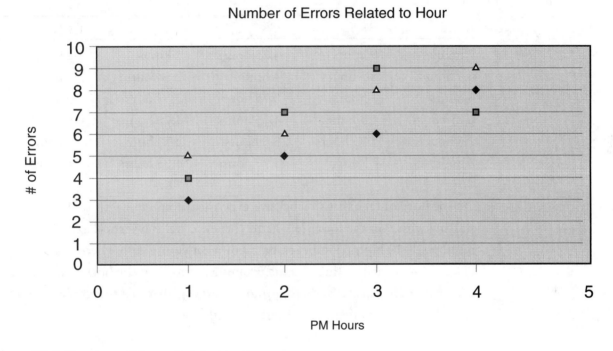

Figure 12.5. Number of Errors Related to Hour

Use the graph in figure 12.5 to answer the following questions.

1. During which hour of the day did the Airsafe Bolt Company observe the most errors in their products?

   a. 12:00 p.m.   b. 2:00 p.m.   c. 4:00 p.m.

2. According to the data in figure 12.5, is it likely that errors increase in the last hours of the workday?

Your Turn

You have been asked to lead the "Family Reads" book week for your children's school. You have decided that you want some data to use to make your points while speaking. Since you want to investigate the possibility of a positive correlation between hours of reading outside the classroom per week with letter grades, you select the scattergram for displaying your data. Your survey gathered information about the reading habits of 30 students. The data gathered from this survey is organized in the following table.

A's	B's	C's	D's	F's
7 hours	5 hours	4.75 hours	2 hours	1.25 hours
6.5 hours	5.5 hours	4 hours	2.5 hours	.75 hours
6 hours	6 hours	3.75 hours	1.5 hours	1.0 hours
6.25 hours	4.5 hours	4.25 hours	1.75 hours	0 hours
7.5 hours	4.75 hours	3.5 hours	2.75 hours	.50 hours
8 hours	4 hours	3.25 hours	1.25 hours	.25 hours

On the horizontal axis (X) label five even measurements with F, D, C, B, and A, starting with F in the lower left-hand corner. Label the vertical axis (Y) with the numbers 1–10 hours. Find each data point on your graph where X and Y cross. Place a dot at each of these points. Example: Find F on the horizontal axis. Find 1.25 on the vertical axis and bring your fingers together in a straight line until they meet. Place a dot at that point. Continue with the rest of the data.

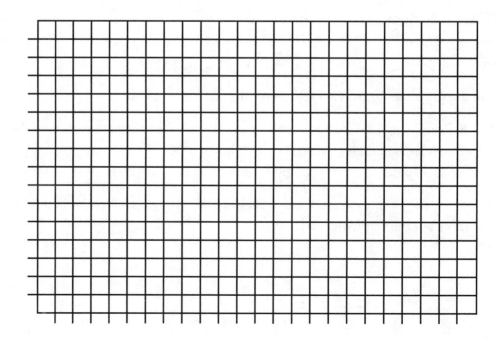

1. Does this scattergram show a positive or a negative correlation?

    _____

2. Will this graph help you make the point you want to make in your presentation? Explain.

    _____

    _____

Chapter 13

Problem Solving with Fishbone Diagrams

In this chapter you will learn to recognize and use a valuable problem-solving tool—the fishbone diagram. This diagram, shaped like a fish skeleton, is one of the better-known problem-solving tools. Knowing how to interpret a fishbone diagram will help you stay ahead of your competition.

Where You Will Find Them

This strange-looking problem-solving tool is easy to recognize because it has the shape of a fish skeleton. Professor Ishikawa, one of the leaders of efforts to improve manufacturing quality in Japan, developed it as a tool to help in organizing ideas about the cause of a problem. For this reason, this diagram is also called the *Ishikawa* diagram.

In the early days of quality-improvement programs, the fishbone diagram was used by all quality circles or process-improvement teams. These were small teams of people in a business, consisting of a leader, a recorder to record ideas, and other team members. The purpose of their meeting was to discover the cause of a specific problem, sometimes called the *effect*, and to find solutions. For this reason, this diagram is called a *cause and effect* diagram. Today, this diagram is used for the same purpose, although the teams are no longer called quality circles—they are called *process improvement teams* or simply *teams*.

> ☀ **When you see a fishbone diagram, think:** The words written on the head of the fish represent the problem. The words on the ribs of the fish could be causing the problem.

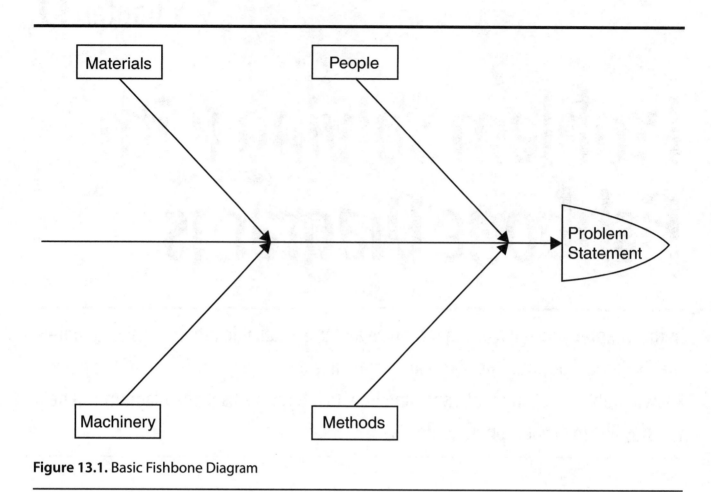

Figure 13.1. Basic Fishbone Diagram

All three names—*Ishikawa, fishbone,* and *cause and effect*—refer to the same basic diagram. In this book, though, we will call it a *fishbone.* The basic diagram starts out with the head of the fish, on which the problem, or effect, is written, and with the spine and four large bones or ribs. Each rib is the organizer for a category of causes. The categories that are most commonly used for this diagram when problem solving in industry are:

- people
- machines
- methods
- material

Other categories can be used if they are more appropriate. Sometimes the team brainstorms ideas first, then groups them together and names each group. These names then go on the ribs of the fish. There can be more than the four ribs if the group identifies more categories. Once all of the contributing causes to a problem are listed, the root cause usually becomes clear.

The fishbone diagram is used early in a problem-solving process. When a team uses a fishbone diagram, its members are able to brainstorm and organize information without becoming emotionally involved with the responses. *Brainstorming* is a process of verbalizing any idea that comes to mind without fear of criticism. It is used to encourage creativity and free thinking, especially when a team is trying to find the cause of a problem. This is usually conducted in an organized way so that ideas can be recorded in front of the team.

A Customer-Service Problem

The Efficiency Executive Suites have been receiving complaints about the phone service, especially the number of lost messages each day. Since telephone service is one of the benefits for tenants in the executive suites, a team has been formed to look into the causes and recommend further action. Figure 13.2 shows the results of their brainstorming session.

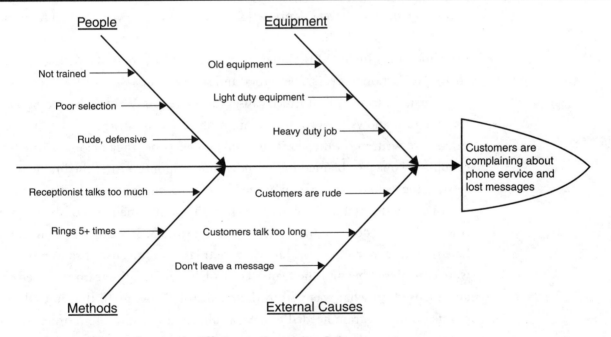

Figure 13.2. Poor Phone Service in Efficiency Executive Suites

After the phone service improvement team met and brainstormed causes for the poor service, they could see several things they could investigate further. Even though these ideas were not new to the team members, putting them on a fishbone diagram clarified which causes should be investigated. In addition to the contributing causes listed in figure 13.2, some other causes were named after the meeting. In which category would you put these causes?

1. Receptionist takes very detailed messages for some calls while others have to wait.

   Category: _____

2. Transfer to voice mail takes 5–6 rings. Clients hang up.

   Category: _____

   Which contributing causes do you think should be investigated further?

   _____

   _____

A Manufacturing Problem

In one manufacturing facility, too many circuit boards were being rejected because of soldering errors. When products are rejected they are called "rejects" and the error is a "defect." A process improvement team was formed to work on this problem, identify the causes, and select some causes to investigate further. The team members included the quality engineers (QE), manufacturing engineers (ME), production workers, inspectors, and supervisors.

First, the team brainstormed causes for the rejects. Writing their responses on the diagram allows the group to remain objective about the causes. (Once the causes are written on the chart in front of everyone, they belong to the whole group—no one gets blamed for an individual response.) After the brainstorming session, the team discussed each of the ideas to see which ones to look into further.

During the first discussion on each of the points, members of the team narrowed 20 points down to the ten shown in figure 13.3. Some of the points initially listed, such as machinery problems, were treated as "givens," meaning that they were considered beyond the team's control. Therefore, the team removed them and focused on what was within their control. They noted that not all of the points on the diagram needed to have a solution or resolution in order to eliminate or reduce the problem.

Within a few two-hour sessions, the team had determined that either a QE or an ME would conduct what they termed a "First-Run Analysis" of all boards. Regardless of how many boards were in a lot, one board would be run and analyzed for defects so that any changes needed in machine settings would be done before the rest of the boards were run.

This change in procedures showed immediate results, reducing defects by more than half within the first week. This example demonstrates how useful it is for entry-level employees to understand and be able to use the fishbone diagram.

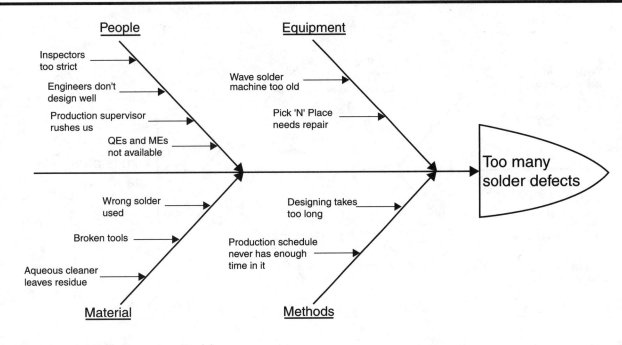

Figure 13.3. A Manufacturing Problem

Use the diagram in figure 13.3 to decide in which category you would put the following.

1. No training

   Category: _____

2. Not enough assemblers

   Category: _____

A Personal Problem

This process can also be useful for an individual. In figure 13.4 you can see the results from someone's personal application of the fishbone diagram. In this example, Tom has a new job and is doing very well except that he is always late to work. His supervisor has talked to him about this and, although Tom stays later than he has to at night, he knows he must correct this problem. In order to find the real cause, he uses the fishbone diagram to help him search for a solution.

In figure 13.4 you can see the results of Tom's soul-searching as he tried to find a reason for being late to work every morning. When Tom organizes his thoughts on paper using a fishbone diagram, he can see several causes for his problem. Some of these causes are things he can fix right away and some of them are things he will have to save money for and plan for.

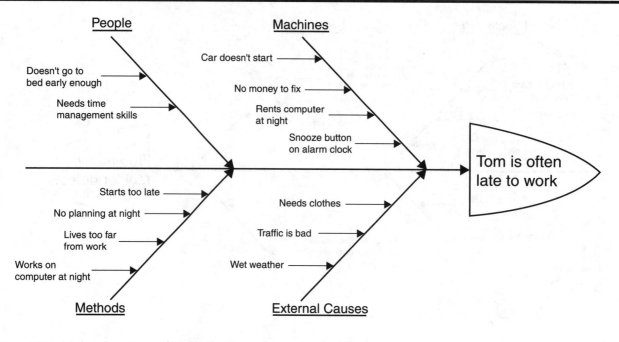

Figure 13.4. Major Causes and Contribution Causes to Problem

Tom thought of two more causes for his lateness. Decide which category each one belongs in.

1. He doesn't allow enough time for the trip plus an unexpected delay.

    Category: _____

2. He has to get gas before he leaves in the morning.

    Category: _____

    Do all of the causes in this diagram seem to be in the correct category?

    _____

Your Turn

The local post office has been delivering mail to the wrong addresses in your area for the last few weeks. Some mail has been sent back to the sender stamped "undeliverable." The people on the mail route are angry with the post office because paychecks have been delayed or sent back. Credit card bills have been sent back to the banks, causing the banks to close accounts. The post office has formed a process-improvement team to determine the source of the problems. The following list of causes was generated during the first brainstorming session. Help the team members by sorting the following items into four major categories and recording them on the fishbone diagram.

Brainstorming List

substitute carrier	addresses not marked on boxes	manual sort
wrong zip codes	no automated equipment	too much junk mail
vicious dogs	no space to sort out mail	not qualified
poor directions	no training	

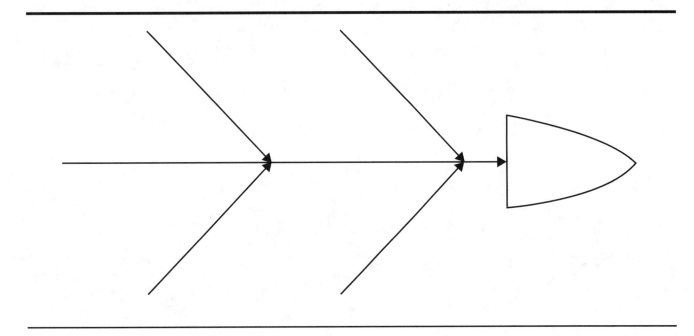

Chapter 14

Go with the Flow

Flowcharts

This chapter will show you how to read and construct flowcharts. These charts are used frequently in all types of businesses. New software is making it easier to construct them on the computer, so you will probably see more and more of them. Being able to read and interpret flowcharts will make you more knowledgeable about workplace communication.

Where You Will Find Them

Flowcharts are graphic displays of step-by-step actions to take in a specific part of a job. You will see them used in the workplace for recording and clarifying steps in work processes and for examining work activities. With flowcharts you can identify all of the steps in a particular job and then discuss which ones are useful and which ones are not. They are very useful as training guides, both for the trainer and for the trainee. When the training session is over, you—the trainee—will have a reminder of the steps to take and the order in which to do them.

> ☀ **When you see a flowchart, think:**
> Here is a step-by-step guide for doing a specific task. This is the order in which I can do it.

You can see that flowcharts are useful for all types of businesses—office, manufacturing, and service. Nonprofit organizations as well as traditional businesses use flowcharts today. If you can read and create flowcharts, either by hand or by computer, you will show your boss that you have some advanced job skills.

Making Pizza

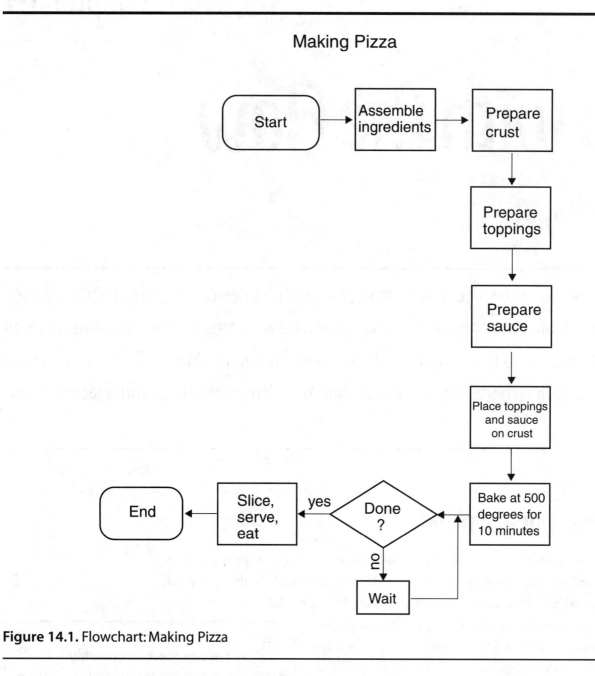

Figure 14.1. Flowchart: Making Pizza

Almost any task can be flowcharted. Some everyday examples would be cooking a special dish, driving a car, using an ATM machine—any activity that can be broken into steps. A flowchart lets you see the individual steps in order and helps you understand them. It lets you identify problem areas such as steps that are out of order or skills that are needed.

If a job process does not have a flowchart, you can impress your supervisor by creating your own, to see if you understand his/her directions. This will improve your performance and show your supervisor that you are making a lot of effort to understand the job.

The good news is that flowcharts are easy to create by hand. Some flowcharts get very complicated but that doesn't make them better than simple ones. Actually, simple is better than complicated when it comes to flowcharts. They should show a sequential flow of activities, clearly, in understandable symbols and language.

What to Look For

the title

Just like other visual displays of information, the first thing to look for is the title of the flowchart. This will tell you the name of the process you are examining.

the connecting lines and arrows

Notice the connecting lines and arrows. The arrows, which indicate the direction or flow of the steps, will tell you how to read the chart.

the graphic symbols

Each of the graphic symbols in the flowchart will be labeled clearly.

The main flowchart symbols that you need to understand are:

Arrows show the direction of the flow or sequence. An arrow points to the next step.

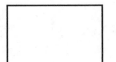

Ovals mean the beginning or the end of the process. They mark the scope, or extent, of the process.

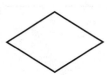

Rectangles represent steps. Each main step is represented by its own rectangle.

Diamonds indicate decision points. A diamond should have one arrow going into it and two arrows going out. If the decision is A, the arrow goes one way. If the decision is B, the arrow goes the other way.

Using Your New Computer

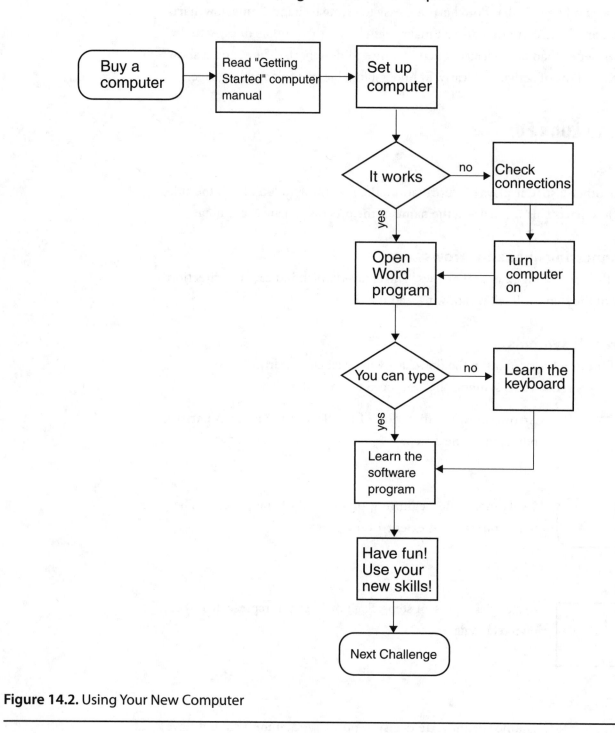

Figure 14.2. Using Your New Computer

Use the flowchart in figure 14.2 to answer the following questions.

1.   What is the process that is flowcharted in figure 14.2?

     _____

2.   Write the label of the first step in the process flowcharted in figure 14.2.

     _____

3.   If you cannot type, what does the chart say to do next?

     _____

4.   What is the final step in using a computer for the first time as described in
      the flowchart?

     _____

5.   Name one way a flowchart is useful.

     _____

Hosting a Party

Richard wanted to have a party in his new house and he wanted to invite some
clients as well as some friends. It seemed like a good idea until he started planning
and found that there were many things to organize in order to have the party run
smoothly. It all seemed very confusing and was beginning to seem more like work
than fun.

Just in time, a friend of his—an experienced party-giver—offered her help.
She sat down with Richard and asked him about the party he wanted to give. Then
she drew a flowchart of steps for him so he could see the process as several small
steps instead of being overwhelmed with everything at once. The flowchart in figure 14.3 is Richard's process for planning and giving the party. What do you think?
Are these the steps you would go through to give a party? What has he left out?

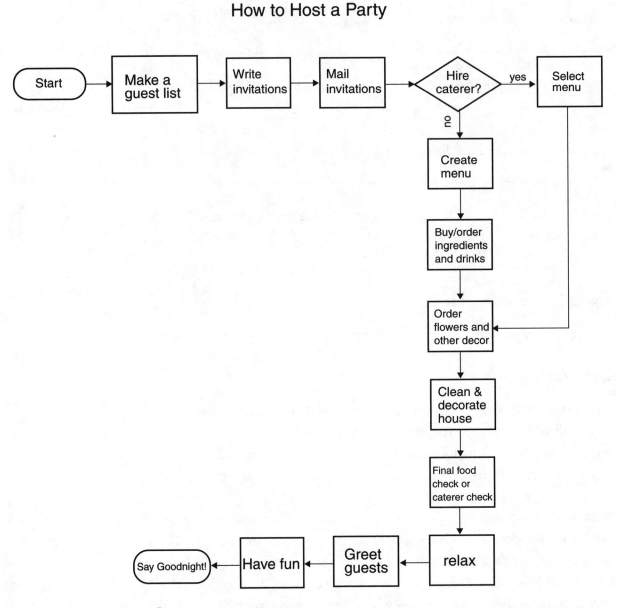

Figure 14.3. How to Host a Party

Use the flowchart in figure 14.3 to answer the following questions.

1. What is the title of this flowchart?

    _____

2. How many steps are there in this process if Richard hires a caterer?

    _____

3. How many steps are there in this process if Richard does not hire a caterer?

_____

4. Name one or two steps that are not on the flowchart.

_____

5. In which of the steps that are shown here is something most likely to go wrong?

_____

Your Turn

Use the symbols that you have learned and flowchart one of the following processes:

1. getting your first driver's license

2. producing a document on a computer

3. giving a speech to a group of people

4. any job that you know how to do, such as:
    —starting and running a machine
    —making a product

Chapter 15

Keep It Moving

Gantt and PERT Charts

This chapter will show you how to read time and activity charts, especially Gantt and PERT charts. These tools help you relate one part of a project to the start and stop dates of another part of the project. By reading these charts, you will be able to see where your activities fit in with the total project.

Where You Will Find Them

Time and activity charts are usually bar charts that are used for displaying events and activities as they relate to a specific amount of time. They are especially useful for showing the impact of individual responsibilities on a whole project or department. Most of these charts show time on the top horizontal axis and people or activities on the vertical axis. Bars are used to show periods of time. These charts are used for scheduling, work assignments, project management, and communicating.

> ☼ **When you see a Gantt chart, think:** Here is a visual display and schedule of the major parts of a project as they relate to each other.

Scheduling Gantt Charts

The idea of displaying vacation time like this may seem very simple to you, but it is the act of making it visible that makes this scheduling technique a valuable tool. People understand the total picture better when there is a visual guide like this. The chart in figure 15.1 shows the Gantt chart in its simplest form.

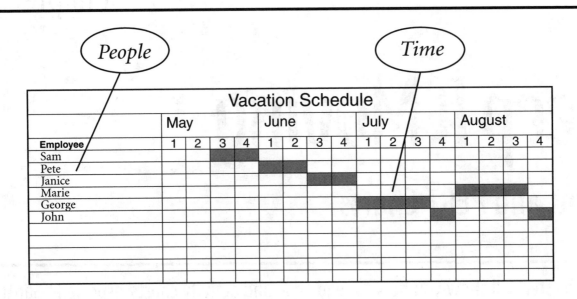

Figure 15.1. Vacation Schedule

Use the chart in figure 15.1 to answer the following questions.

1. Who is taking his or her vacation in two separate weeks?

_____

2. Which two employees are taking three weeks of vacation?

_____

3. How many employees will be working in this group from the third week in May until the last of August?

_____

Project Planning Gantt Charts

The Gantt chart is a visual tool that displays the timeframe for each part of a project and how it fits with the other parts of the project. This allows the project team members to keep their part of the project on schedule—or to acknowledge when they are not on schedule. This type of visual display is very useful when there are multiple tasks to be done and each sequential task depends on the one that came before it.

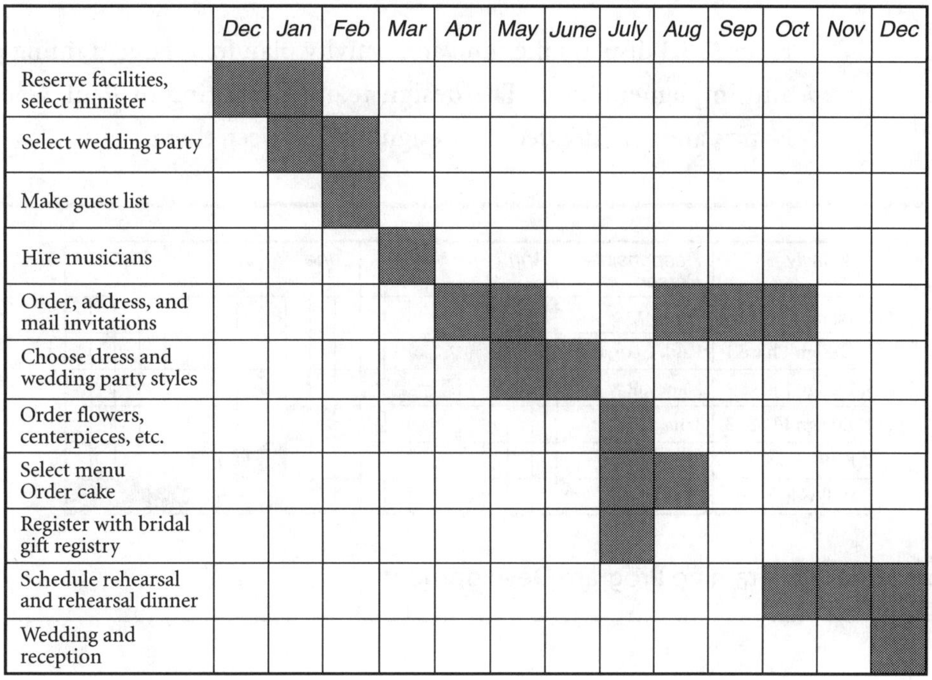

	Dec	Jan	Feb	Mar	Apr	May	June	July	Aug	Sep	Oct	Nov	Dec
Reserve facilities, select minister	■	■											
Select wedding party		■	■										
Make guest list			■										
Hire musicians				■									
Order, address, and mail invitations					■	■			■	■	■		
Choose dress and wedding party styles						■	■						
Order flowers, centerpieces, etc.								■					
Select menu Order cake								■	■				
Register with bridal gift registry								■					
Schedule rehearsal and rehearsal dinner											■	■	■
Wedding and reception													■

Figure 15.2. Gantt Chart for Wedding Planning

Use the chart in figure 15.2 to answer the following questions.

1. When are the invitations scheduled to be mailed?

   _____

2. Which month has the most activities scheduled?

   _____

3. Which activity is extended for the longest period of time?

   _____

Training Program Gantt Charts

Figure 15.3 displays the time and activity plan for a large training program design and implementation. The design team, consisting of Paul, George, Lisa, Jane, Nancy, and Ray, divided the design task between them.

Activity	Responsible Person	April	May	June	July	August
Plan project	Team	■				
Design Phase 1	Paul, George		■			
Design Phase 2	Nancy, Ray		■			
Design Phase 3	Jane, Lisa			■		
RER*	Team				■	
Roll-out	Trainers					■

Figure 15.3. Gantt Chart for Training Program Development

Use the chart in figure 15.3 to answer the following questions.

1. Who is responsible for planning the project?

   _____

2. In which month does design phase 2 begin?

   _____

3. During the RER activity, are the team members working on any other part of the project?

   _____

4. Which activities overlap?

   _____

One use for the Gantt chart is to show tasks that have to be done at the same time. Another use is to show tasks that depend on a previous task and therefore must be done sequentially. Each activity is displayed according to start date and end date. Actually, each of the subactivities could be displayed on a separate Gantt chart. As the tasks are implemented, you can show the progress of each on the chart. That way, if one person is behind schedule, the whole team gets that information and can adjust their schedules so that they will be ready at the right time and downtime can be kept to a minimum.

Process Improvement Project Gantt Chart

Figure 15.4 shows an actual Gantt chart for a continuous improvement project in a manufacturing plant. This process-improvement project was first mentioned in chapter 13 when you learned about fishbone diagrams. The team used the fishbone to help them find the cause of the soldering problem. After the problem was identified, they planned the improvement project with the help of the following Gantt chart. They could then look at the timeframe for the total project and be able to schedule individual activities.

In figure 15.4, the major activities needed to complete the project are identified. Note that not all activities start at the same time.

Use the chart in figure 15.4 to answer the following questions.

1.   When is the proposal scheduled to be ready for executive approval?

Action/Activity	Jan	Feb	Mar	Apr	May	June	July
Conduct first runs on all lots and collect data	▓	▓	▓	▓	▓	▓	▓
Determine cost of replacing wave solder	▓	▓					
Repair Pick N Place machine	▓		▓				
Prepare proposal for executive approval		▓	▓				
Certify two in-house trainers				▓			
Train all production employees					▓	▓	▓

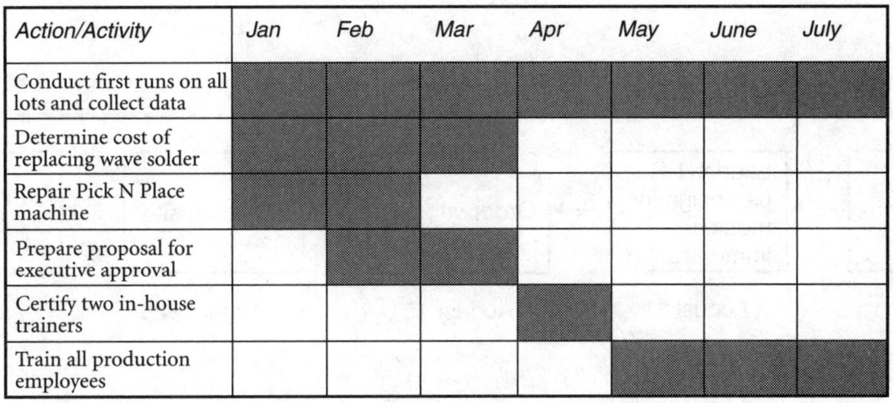

Figure 15.4. Gantt Chart for Solder Improvement Project

2. What is the activity that is scheduled to be completed just before the training starts?

    _____

3. Which month has the most activities scheduled to be going on at one time?

    _____

The PERT Chart

The Program Evaluation Review Technique chart, or PERT chart, is really a Gantt chart in the form of a flow chart. Arrows show the flow of steps and the target dates are written under the rectangles that house each step. This type of chart provides a visual display of the activities, the order in which they are to be done, and the expected completion dates. This lets everyone view each step in the project and how it fits into the overall picture.

Figure 15.5 shows a PERT chart for an immunization campaign conducted by an HMO. They provide this service for their members every year, but last year there was a poor turnout. They thought that the main cause was that no one knew about the program. This year they wanted to improve the turnout so they planned the action steps using a PERT chart. The planning team meets once a week to review their progress on meeting their schedule.

Use the chart in figure 15.5 to answer the following questions.

1. How many days after the PR campaign is launched will the HMO do the immunizations?

    _____

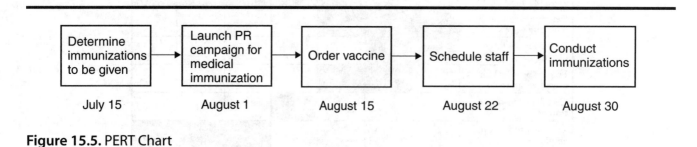

Determine immunizations to be given	Launch PR campaign for medical immunization	Order vaccine	Schedule staff	Conduct immunizations
July 15	August 1	August 15	August 22	August 30

Figure 15.5. PERT Chart

2.   How many weeks before the immunization day is the vaccine supposed to be ordered?

_____

Your Turn

Your child's competitive soccer team is starting a new season and you have been asked to help organize the team and manage the activity assignment and implementation. In the past, there have been problems because things were not done on time. You want to plan all of the activities on the Gantt chart below. The major activities to be planned are:

- hold tryouts
- select team
- hold parent meeting
- set up practices
- practice
- enter tournaments (paperwork, applications, etc.)
- order uniforms (2-week turnaround)
- play games

Soccer Season Gantt Chart										
Action/Activity	March	April	May	June	July	Aug	Sept	Oct	Nov	Dec

Tryouts run for one week in April. Games begin in June and go through September. Congratulations! You are ready to enjoy the soccer season.

Chapter 16

Who's Who and What's What

Tree Diagrams and Organization Charts

In this chapter you will learn to recognize and read a useful tool, the *tree diagram*. Interpreting tree diagrams will allow you to read large organizational plans and create detailed plans for your own work area. You will be able to find the main goal of the diagram quickly as well as all of the steps needed to achieve that goal.

Where You Will Find Them

You will find tree diagrams used in community recreation programs, science, computer science, management meetings, and anywhere there is a need to organize information into a logical hierarchy. Ellen R. Domb, in her December 1994 article "Seven New Tools: The Ingredients for Successful Problem Solving" from *Quality Digest*, explains tree diagrams very well: These diagrams begin or end with a single entry that is the main goal or the main topic. This single entry is broken into at least two goals or subcategories that are broken into two goals or subcategories each. Each time a category is divided it becomes more detailed. The trunk of the

> **When you see a tree diagram, think:** All of the people or things on the branches came from or are related to the first thing on the trunk of the tree.

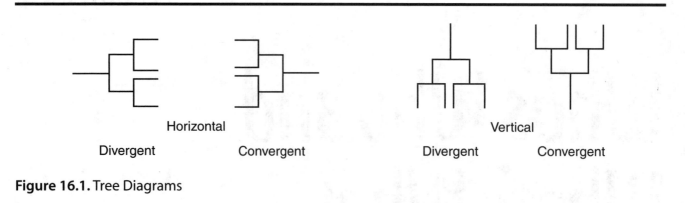

Figure 16.1. Tree Diagrams

tree is the major goal or main category. Branches are major options, twigs are components of the options, and leaves are all the different ways to accomplish the options.

You read horizontal tree diagrams from left to right and vertical tree diagrams from top to bottom. Sometimes you start reading at the single entry and read through the multiple entries—*divergent*. Sometimes you start with the multiple entries and move toward the single entry—*convergent*.

Family Trees

One familiar tree diagram is the *family tree*. The purpose of making a family tree is to create a logical display of family ancestry as far back as you can. Since this information doubles at each entry, it can be a large task. The family tree keeps the information organized and easy to understand because it is a visual organization. Creating family tree diagrams has become even more popular and easier with the availability of research sources on the Internet.

Figure 16.2 is an example of a horizontal divergent tree diagram. The information is, of course, fictitious, but it shows how you could construct your own family tree by using a tree diagram.

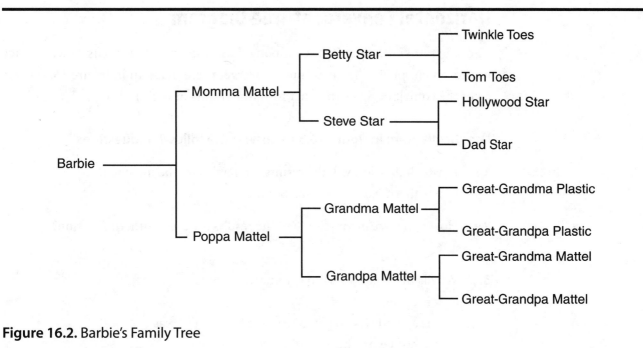

Figure 16.2. Barbie's Family Tree

Use the diagram in figure 16.2 to answer the following questions.

1.   Who were the great-grandparents on Poppa Mattel's side?

     _____

2.   Who were the great-grandmothers on Momma Mattel's side of the family?

     _____

Horizontal Convergent Tree Diagram

The CustomersRImportant Company has implemented a customer-service improvement plan. The horizontal convergent tree diagram in Figure 16.3 shows all of the contributing factors that form the results of their research.

Use the diagram in figure 16.3 to answer the following questions.

1. In which division will the results for Territory 1 be included?
    a. Northern   b. Southern

2. How many areas contribute to the results for the Southern Division?
    a. 6   b. 4   c. 8

3. Why is this a good way to summarize results?
    a. it is easier to count
    b. it is a good way to get information from all areas
    c. it keeps people busy

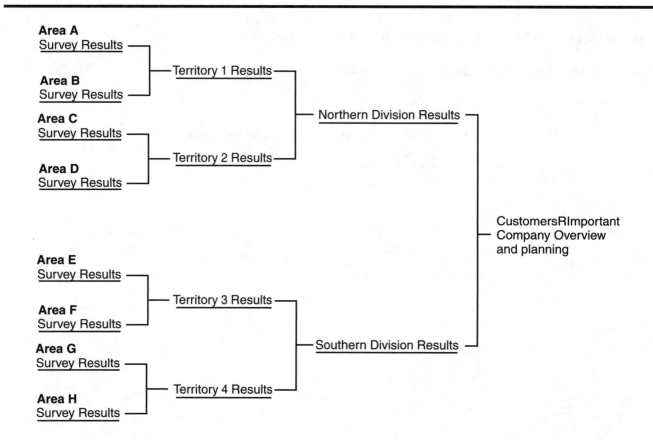

Figure 16.3. Improving Customer Service

Vertical Convergent Tree Diagram

The community college regional basketball association is having a tournament and the schedule is posted in the form of a vertical convergent tree diagram. It's easy to read, and you can go back to it often to visualize your team in first place!

Use the diagram in figure 16.4 to answer the following questions.

1. At what time does the winner of round one between teams C and D play the winner of the A and B game?

   _____

2. What is the day and the time of the final game?

   _____

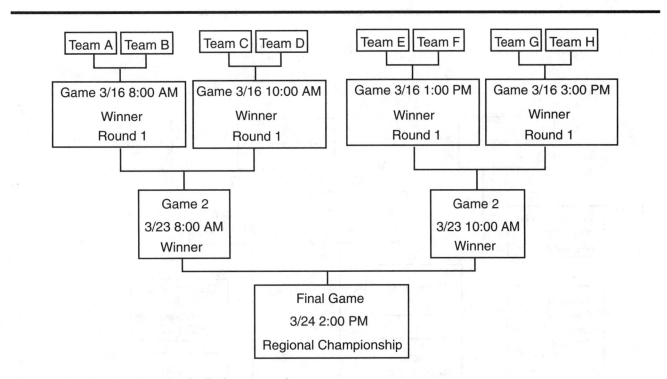

Figure 16.4. Regional Basketball Championships

Vertical Divergent Tree Diagram

You can use the tree diagram to break down a major task or objectives into subtasks. Each subtask should be a way to accomplish the major objective. The objectives should be ways to accomplish the main goal. Using the tree diagram this way is a way to make goals, objectives, and action steps visible. Then you can check your action steps to make sure they are the right things to do in order to reach the major objective.

The diagram in 16.5 shows the results of a planning session that investigated the possibility of buying Grandma a Ferrari for Christmas. The desired outcome or goal is listed at the top of the diagram. The possible avenues for getting enough money are listed under the first entry. Each of these possibilities is at the same level: They could either save money, earn money, or borrow money. The brainstorming has continued on each of these ideas.

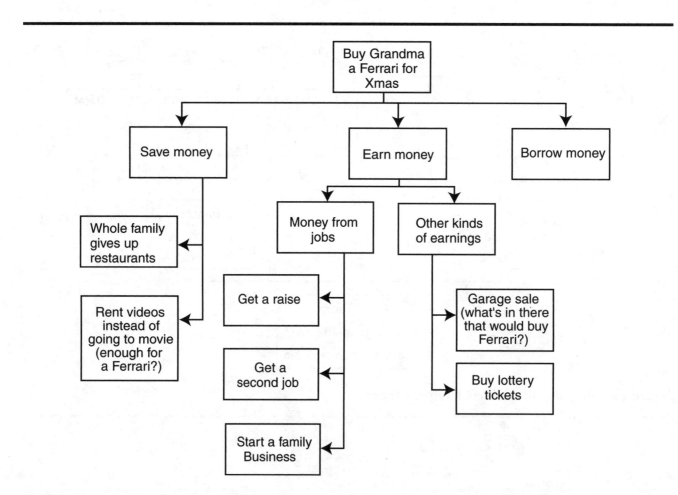

Figure 16.5. Buy Grandma a Ferrari for Xmas

Use the diagram in figure 16.5 to answer the following questions.

1. Which of the major objectives has no action steps identified for it?

   _____

2. Which major objective splits into two possible action steps?

   _____

Organization Charts

Organization charts show how departments, people, equipment, or functions of an organization are related to one another and how they are positioned or arranged in the company. The names of each component are usually enclosed in a box or some type of geometric shape. They are then grouped together according to reporting patterns and are connected with lines and arrows. One type of organization chart shows an overview of a company, such as in figure 16.6. Here you see the way the company is organized into smaller parts.

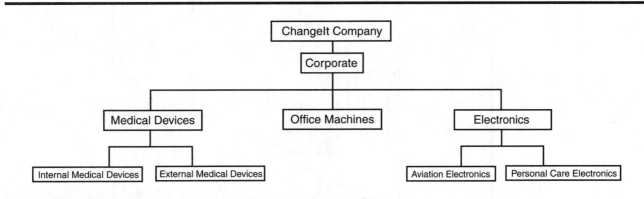

Figure 16.6. Organizational Chart by Major Organizational Units

Organizational charts that show titles and functions are the ones with which we are most familiar. These charts show reporting relationships and titles for individuals. You can find out a lot about the organization by studying this chart. Are the positions closest to the president the director, senior vice president, or vice president positions? How many vice presidents do they have? Where is your boss on this chart? Is he at the bottom? Is he not on the chart at all? Who does he report to? All of this information tells you more about your job.

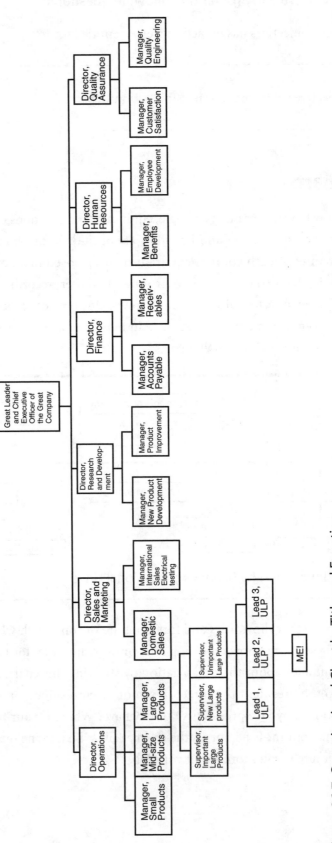

Figure 16.7. Organizational Chart by Title and Function

Use the chart in figure 16.7 to answer the following questions.

1. To whom does the manager of midsize products report?

   _____

2. To whom does the director of research and development report?

   _____

3. Which director of the company has responsibility for customer satisfaction?

   _____

4. To which supervisor do you report?

   _____

Your Turn

Organize the following information on the blank tree diagram below. Your major goal is to relocate to Utopia, Hawaii within the next six months. Four objectives that have to be achieved in order to make that dream come true are:

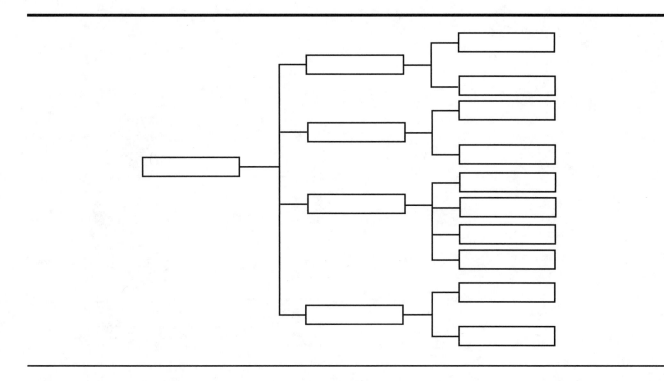

- organize current business to sustain itself when you are not there
  1. hire and train instructors
  2. standardize systems that can be duplicated

- make contacts and establish business in Utopia
  1. conduct public relations activities in Utopia
     a. phone survey
     b. write article for local publication
     c. send letters re: results of survey
  2. join professional organizations in Utopia
     a. attend monthly meetings
     b. network

- create a financial cushion to cover the move
  1. save money
  2. pay off credit cards
  3. estimate costs
  4. audit existing accounts

- simplify move
  1. have garage sale
  2. clean files

Chapter 17

Blueprints 101

Blueprints and Drawings

This chapter will prove to you that you don't have to be an engineer to read a blueprint. You will be able to find information on the print and interpret all those different views of an object. If you like to draw, you may even find a new career in these pages!

Where You'll Find Them

Prints are the way that product designers communicate with the people who make the product. Prints state the specifications, show responsibilities for drawing, and give the production workers a guide for their job. Every part of an airplane is manufactured to a print. Water sprinklers are manufactured to the specifications on prints. Circuit boards and satellite harnesses are manufactured to print specifications. Cars, boats, and other vehicles begin with prints.

> When you see a blueprint or a print, **think:** Here are exact directions for making a part or a product.

Actually, you may never see a blueprint in a manufacturing plant, but you will see lots of prints. Blueprints were developed as a visual communication tool for manufacturing. As products became more and more mass produced and the individual designer lost control over the production of the product, there had to be a way to communicate uniform directions to others. For this purpose, blueprints were developed.

The engineer first made a drawing of each part of the whole product. This was very time consuming and costly. In order to get this drawing into the hands of production managers, copies had to be made. These first prints were called *blueprints* because they were blue with white lines on them. The term blueprint became so widely used that today it means all kinds of drawing reproductions. The terms print, blueprint, whiteprint, diazo print, industrial print, and drawing are all names of copies that are used in the shop.

Prints are the graphic language of manufacturing. They contain information that is very detailed and would be hard to communicate with words alone. Production departments control and manage all areas with the help of prints. Prints contain the specific directions, measurements, and other technical information. They are exact copies of the engineering drawing and they are made to be used in the shop.

How to Read a Print

The first place to look for information is the *title block*. This is a rectangle that contains other rectangles. It organizes the general information about the object in the drawing or print. The company that makes the print decides what information in the title block should be. Because of this, title blocks may be quite different from print to print. Usually the title block is found in the lower right-hand corner of the drawing. It is the key to interpreting prints.

The Title Block

1. NAME AND ADDRESS
This block shows the name and location of the manufacturer who created the drawing.

2. TITLE
This block gives a short description of the object in the drawing.

3. PART NUMBER
This block lists the number of the part in the body of the drawing.

4. DRAWING NUMBER
This number identifies the drawing number instead of the part number. There may be more than one part on a drawing.

5. DRAWN BY/DATE
This section has the name of the person who did the drawing and the date he/she finished it.

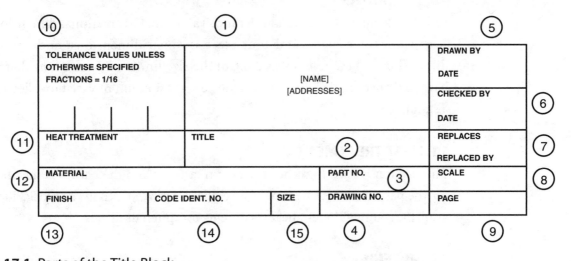

Figure 17.1. Parts of the Title Block

6. CHECKED BY/DATE

The person who checks the drawing for accuracy signs here and dates the drawing.

7. REPLACES/REPLACED BY

This block records the number of the parts that either replace or are replaced by the part in the print. If it is supposed to replace another part, the old part number is recorded in the REPLACES block. If the part shown is replaced by a newer part, the new part number is recorded in the REPLACED BY block.

8. SCALE

Scale tells you how much like the real part the drawing is. Is it the same size as the part? Then the scale will be 1:1. If the part is ¼:1, then it is ¼ the size of the actual part.

9. PAGE

The page block shows the number the page is in the sequence of pages and the last number shows the total number of pages in the drawing. Example: Page 1 of 4 or page 2 of 4.

10. TOLERANCES

This block shows the general tolerance values for (a) fractional dimensions; (b) two-place, three-place, and four-place decimal dimensions; and (c) angular dimensions. These tolerances control the size limits of dimensions that do not have tolerance applied directly. (tolerance = the amount of variation allowed from a standard)

11. HEAT TREATMENT

This section is used to record the heat treatment and the hardness specifications for the part. If no heat treatment is required, write NONE in the block. Tables are available stating different heat treatments for different metals.

12. MATERIAL

The material to be used for this part is described by name and number. No other material should be used unless you get proper authorization.

13. FINISH

This section describes the appearance of the finished part. Special finishes will be written here or on the body of the print.

14. CODE IDENTIFICATION NUMBER

This is the number the government assigns to the company.

15. SIZE

This is the size of the drawing.

TOLERANCE VALUES UNLESS OTHERWISE SPECIFIED FRACTIONS = +1/32				BETTER MACHINING COMPANY NORTH HOLLYWOOD CALIFORNIA	DRAWN BY J. Smith
					DATE 9-4-99
.xx	.xxx	.xxxx	Angles		CHECKED BY A. Blind
+ .01	+ .002	+ .0002	+0-30		DATE 9-4-99
HEAT TREATMENT HDN to Rc58			TITLE Bracket		REPLACES ---------
					REPLACED BY --------
MATERIAL SA 1280 Steel				PART NO. 865340-2	SCALE Full
FINISH Noted	CODE IDENT. NO. 01256.6		SIZE C	DRAWING NO. E-5163-1-4	PAGE 1 of 2

Figure 17.2. Title Block

Use the graphic in figure 17.2 to answer the following questions.

1. What is the name of the part?

    _____

2. What is the number of the part?

    _____

3. What is the sheet page?

    _____

4. How many sheets are in the complete set?

    _____

5. Who did the drawing?

    _____

6. When did he/she finish it?

    _____

7. What material is specified for the part?

    _____

8. What heat treatment is required for this part?

    _____

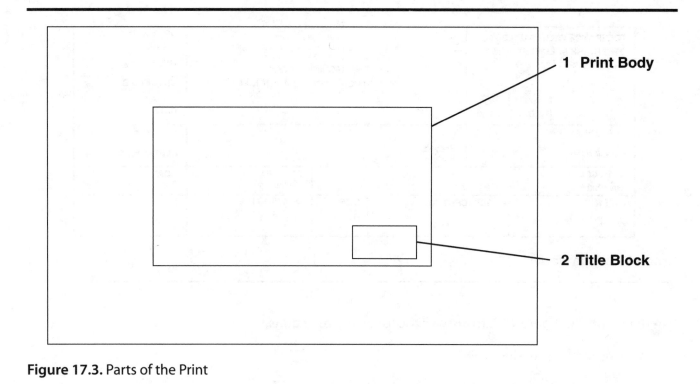

Figure 17.3. Parts of the Print

Print Body

The print body is the main part of the drawing; it may show one or more views of the object. A photograph may show what the object looks like, but it cannot show the detail that viewing it from different angles can provide, such as dimensions and angles. For this reason, the print shows different views.

You can understand this better if you take a piece of paper and a pencil and draw a chest of drawers as you look at it from the front. Then move to the side and draw what you see. Now move to the back and draw that view. Finally, stand over the chest of drawers and draw it looking down on it from the top. Did you see the same thing each time?

Reading Different Views

Multiview prints help you visualize the part by giving specific details about every view. Each view helps you visualize the shape of the part. The *dimensions*, or measurements, are on the print. Dimensions and scale help you visualize the size of the part. Tolerances tell you how accurately the measurements have to be followed. A lot of this important information comes from the customer and defines what they will or will not accept.

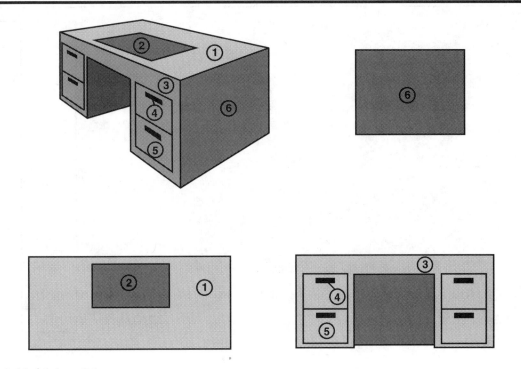

Figure 17.4. Multiview Prints

Your Turn

Try drawing a simple object such as a stapler, a battery charger, a portable phone, or any rectangular object. (Circular objects are harder to draw, so a rectangular one will be easier.)

Take your object and draw different views of it. One view should be pictorial as though it is a photo. One view is top only. One view is side only. One view is front only. Label each view and number the corresponding sides to match the parts on the pictorial.

Now, fill in the title block with the necessary information. Since it's your design, you can write anything you want in the title block. Make any notes on the drawing that would help someone take your drawing and make the part by looking at the drawing.

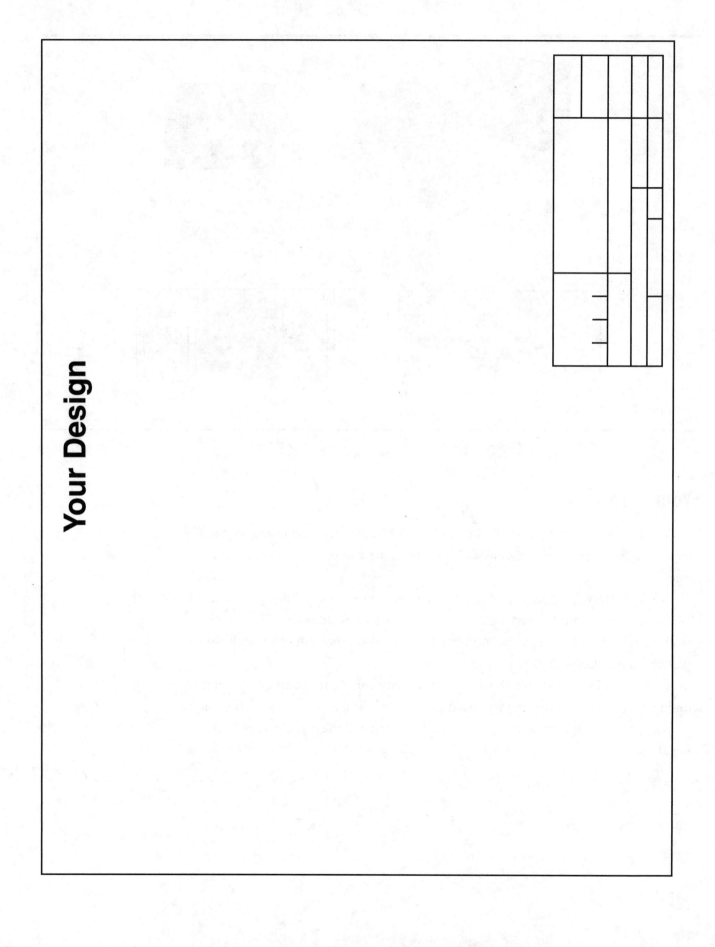

Your Design

Chapter 18

Schematics 101

Electronic Diagrams and Symbols

This chapter will give you an overview of electronic diagrams and introduce you to the symbols used in drawing them. The electronic schematic is a useful tool for building or repairing any electronic circuit, from the simplest light bulb and switch to the most sophisticated integrated circuit. While complicated circuits are designed by engineers, you can learn to design simple circuits and to read the designs of others.

Where You Will Find Them

You may have the chance to work in the field of electricity or electronics since this field is expanding constantly and offers many job opportunities. These opportunities can be found in the areas of electrical engineering, integrated circuits, electronics engineering, systems engineering, electronic data processing, electric utilities, radar, lasers for communication and fiber optics systems for the telephone industry, new forms of power generation equipment, television, radio, appliance repair, and the broadcast industry. With each new technological advance come new applications for electronics and new opportunities for you.

> **When you see a schematic, think:** This diagram shows a combination of parts that are connected to form a circuit path along which electrons can move.

There are several different options for starting out in this field. The strongest start, of course, is a bachelor's degree in electronic engineering. Another suggestion is to get an AA degree with a specialty in electronics from a community college—this too will give you an excellent chance of getting a good job in this field. Your educational background is important, but practical experience is important too. You might want to begin in an entry-level position in an electronics division of a company and see if you enjoy the work.

Schematics are the tools used by engineers to communicate electronic designs and directions to the production workers. Reading schematics is the place to begin if you're going right into the job market. Schematics are to the electronics industry what blueprints are to the manufacturing industry.

Schematics

The schematic diagram is the standard method of communication for electricity and electronics. It shows all of the components of a circuit and how they are connected. You can use it to follow the operation of the circuit from start to finish. The schematic diagram is used by the engineers and technicians during circuit design, construction, and maintenance. It is used in electronics the same way that the blueprint is used in manufacturing and construction.

Schematics use symbols for the different components of a circuit instead of showing drawings of the component. Because these symbols are small, the diagram can be depicted small. The symbols and lines on the schematic show how the parts of the circuit are connected, the order in which they are used, and the way they relate to each other electrically. This makes the schematic a useful tool for anyone who works with electronics.

In figure 18.1 you can see that the schematic is simple to follow. You can read it from left to right in the direction of any arrows. You can probably also see that in order to understand what you're following, you need to be able to interpret the symbols.

Symbols and Letters

You will usually find a symbol for chassis, frame connection, or common ground on a schematic. This symbol stands for a common circuit return to a structure such as a frame for a land, air, or space vehicle that is *not* connected to the ground (examples of these vehicles would include a car, train, airplane, or satellite). However, if the circuit has a direct connection to the ground or to a body of water,

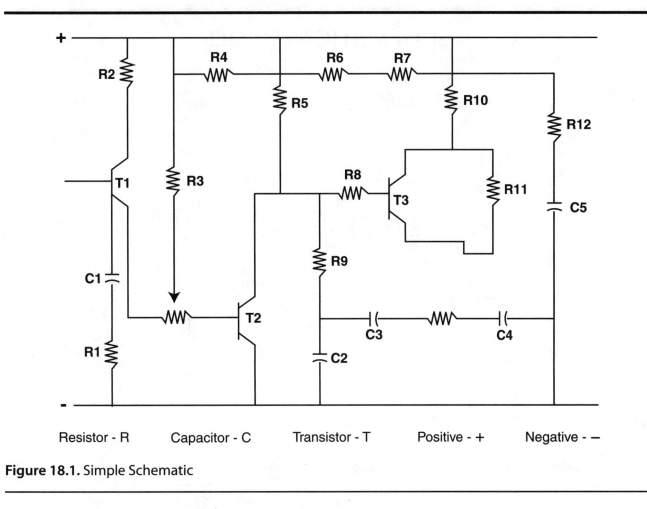

Resistor - R   Capacitor - C   Transistor - T   Positive - +   Negative - —

Figure 18.1. Simple Schematic

more information will be given on the schematic. On a complex circuit board, such as one for television or radio, there will be several common return symbols. This makes it possible to show all connecting points without complicating the schematic with extra lines.

Other common symbols used for components on schematics are shown in figure 18.2. Complete lists of symbols used in electronics are available from the American National Standards Institute (ANSI). ANSI is the organization that is responsible for standardizing these and other symbols for electronics. They also are responsible for standards in other technical fields.

SCHEMATIC SYMBOLS

Alternating-Current source

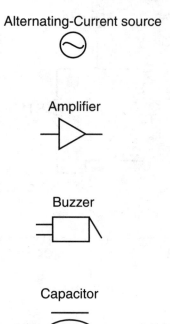

Meter

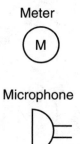

Amplifier

Microphone

Buzzer

Potentiometer, variable resistor

Capacitor

Terminal

Connector, 2 conductor, non-polarized

Transformer, with iron core

Fuse

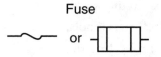 or

Transistor, n-p-n

Ground, general

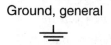

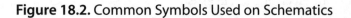

Figure 18.2. Common Symbols Used on Schematics

In addition to components identified by symbols, they are also identified by class designation letters. Some of the main designation letters are:

R   Resistors
C   Capacitors
Q   Transistors

Others include:

AR	Amplifier (non-rotating)	**R**	Potentiometer
BT	Battery		Resistor
	Solar cell		Rheostat
D or	Crystal diode	**S**	Contactor
CR	Metallic rectifier		Disconnecting device
	Varactor		Switch
DS	Alphanumeric display device		Telegraph key
	Light-emitting solid state device		Thermostat
	Signal Light	**V**	Electron tube
HT	Earphones		Phototube
	Electrical headset		Voltage regulator
	Telephone receiver		
Q	Semiconductor controlled rectifier		
	Phototransistor (three terminals)		
	Transistor		

The letters will often be used with numbers when several components of the same kind are used. These are usually shown on the schematic but if they are not, they will be identified in the notes that came with the diagram.

Other Diagrams to Look For

Although the schematic is the most common type of diagram used in electronics, there are several other types of diagrams that are used to show electrical circuits.

Pictorial diagrams

These diagrams are pictures of the components of a circuit. They show how the components connect and relate to each other. You will almost always find them in do-it-yourself kits, and you can use them to guide you in building and repairing the circuit. You will also find them used in manufacturing to show what the product looks like.

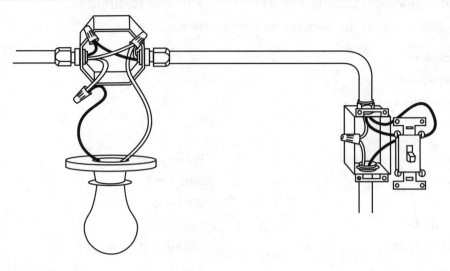

Figure 18.3. Pictorial Diagram

Wiring or connection diagrams

Wiring diagrams are used to show circuit-system connections in a simple way. They are often used with home appliances and automobile electrical systems. These diagrams show the components of a circuit in drawings, and the components are usually identified by name. The positions of the components are shown as they relate to each other. Sometimes the wires are identified by colors, a process referred to as *color coding*.

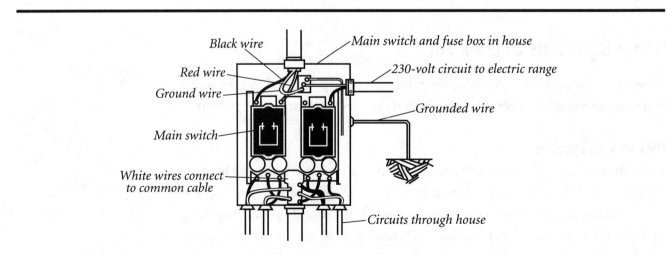

Figure 18.4. Wiring Diagram

Block diagrams

Block diagrams simplify information about complex electrical systems. These diagrams look a lot like the flowcharts that you studied in chapter 14. You read them from left to right in the direction of the arrows. The wires and individual components are not shown on a block diagram.

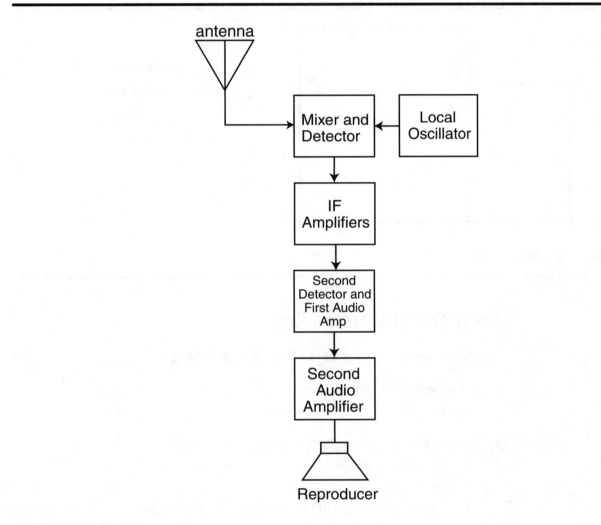

Figure 18.5. Block Diagram

Architectural floor plan diagrams

Architects, electrical designers, and contractors use floor-plan diagrams to show where the parts of a building's electrical system will be located. The contractor's working drawing or blueprint shows the wiring and the conduit system as well as outlets, switches, and lighting fixtures.

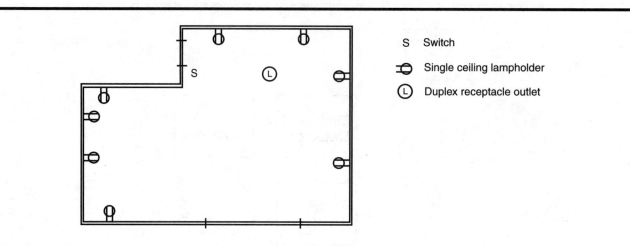

S   Switch

Single ceiling lampholder

(L)   Duplex receptacle outlet

Figure 18.6. Simple Room Design

Check Your Understanding

Select the correct answer to the following questions.

1.   A schematic shows the components as
      a. pictures   b. symbols   c. blocks

2.   An architectural floor plan diagram shows
      a. colors of electrical outlets
      b. light fixtures
      c. location of the parts of the building's electrical system

3.   A simple way to show information about a complicated electrical system is the
      a. block diagram   b. wiring diagram   c. schematic diagram

4.   A schematic drawing shows
      a. the operation of a circuit from beginning to end
      b. a complex electrical system
      c. location of parts of a building's electrical system

Your Turn

On the following schematic diagram, place letters for the following components next to their corresponding symbols.

(1) Resistor 1 (R1)
(2) Resistor 2 (R2)
(3) Diode (D)
(4) Connector plug
(5) Transformer (T)
(6) Capacitor 1 (C1)
    Capacitor 2 (C2)

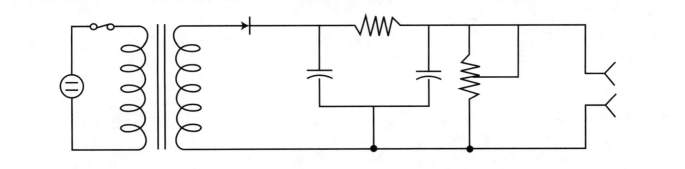

Chapter 19

What You See Is What You Get

Spatial/Visual Intelligence

This chapter reviews ways to increase your spatial/visual intelligence or acuity through fun exercises in visual perception. This will not only increase your visual literacy—it's guaranteed to improve your daydreams!

Why It's Important

Spatial/visual intelligence is highly developed in architects, builders, designers, artists, mapmakers, and engineers. It is the ability to visualize objects, move them around in space, and find your way through space by navigating and exploring. Spatial/visual intelligence increases your ability to read graphics easily.

Some of the world's greatest scientists developed their ideas in the spatial/visual domain rather than the mathematical or linguistic. Einstein thought in terms of images. He carried out experiments in his mind with the use of those images. Many historians believe that the scientific progress in the Renaissance can be tied to the recording and communicating of a huge body of knowledge in drawings. An example of this is the work

> *"Whilst part of what we perceive comes through our senses from the object before us, another part (and it may be the larger part) always comes out of our own mind."*
>
> —William James
>
> *"We see the world not as it is but as we are."* —Anaïs Nin

of Leonardo da Vinci. He used drawings to show the relationships and organization of machines and organisms since they were not available for inspection.

Individuals who are gifted in spatial/visual intelligence can perform in several of the physical sciences and arts. Like da Vinci, one could perform in science, engineering, architecture, and the arts. For others, thinking in three-dimensional images is like learning a foreign language. But it *can* be learned.

Spatial/visual intelligence is one of eight intelligences defined by Howard Gardner in his research at Harvard University. Until this groundbreaking work by Gardner, intelligence was measured by assessment instruments that measured linear linguistic and logical intelligence as demonstrated in the scholastic subjects of math and English. Yet, no one could argue that the great artists of the world were not intelligent.

According to Gardner, an individual may have several types of intelligence that are more developed than the others. This theory may explain why certain individuals who are very accomplished in one area, and find two or three other ways of learning to be interesting and fun, can find the usual linguistic or math areas difficult. They are intelligent, but in different ways from how we are accustomed to defining intelligence.

The eight intelligences as defined by Gardner are:

- spatial/visual intelligence
- linguistic intelligence
- musical intelligence
- logical-mathematical intelligence
- bodily-kinesthetic intelligence
- intrapersonal intelligence (self-knowledge)
- interpersonal intelligence (understanding others)
- naturalist intelligence

Another important point that Gardner makes is that each intelligence can be increased. This chapter reviews exercises and activities that will increase spatial/visual intelligence or ability. Many of these activities are found in your everyday routine. For example, the visual puzzle of "How many rabbits can you find in the tree?" or some variation is often found on children's placemats at restaurants, or even on the back of a cereal box. Twenty years ago you didn't see so many of these puzzles, but today there is much more awareness of the value these exercises have for training spatial/visual intelligence.

For some of you, reading graphics may not come very easily. Perhaps visual exercises were not presented in school or at home, and you did not have the opportunity to work on these skills as you were growing up. Perhaps you watched too much television instead of spending time on other visual activities such as drawing, building models, or solving jigsaw puzzles. You may find some of the exercises in this chapter difficult or frustrating, but don't give up. The good news is, you can increase your spatial/visual intelligence by working on activities similar to the ones you'll find here.

Some exercises that you can try on your own that increase spatial/visual intelligence are:

- copying a form
- matching one form to another
- identifying a form when it is turned in space
- seeing a form or space from a different viewpoint
- drawing while looking at an object
- drawing from memory
- building shapes with "tangram" puzzles (available at any game store; an excellent commercial puzzle is "Tangoes")
- the Japanese art of "origami" or paper folding (books on origami are available at any bookstore, game store, or library)

If you practice looking at objects, scenes, or diagrams and then try re-creating them on paper, with and without looking, you will begin to see details and remember them. Many of us go through the day without really seeing the people or things around us. This type of seeing comes from practice and from training ourselves to focus on detail. Even then, our eyes can fool us, as you'll see in this first exercise!

Illusions

Use figure 19.1 to answer the following questions.

1. How many women are there in figure 19.1a?

    _____

2. Do you see a young woman or an old woman?

    _____

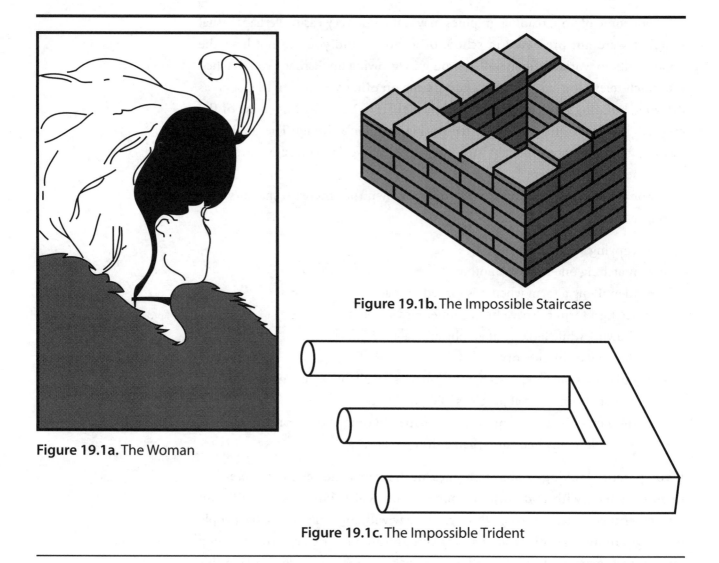

Figure 19.1a. The Woman

Figure 19.1b. The Impossible Staircase

Figure 19.1c. The Impossible Trident

3.   In 19.1b, where is the highest step on the staircase?

_____

4.   In 19.1b, where is the lowest step on the staircase?

_____

5.   Can you draw The Impossible Trident? When you draw it, what do you notice?

_____

Perceptual Awareness

Use figure 19.2 to answer the following questions.

1. Circle the two figures that are exactly alike.

2. How are the other two figures different from the two that are alike?

   _____

   _____

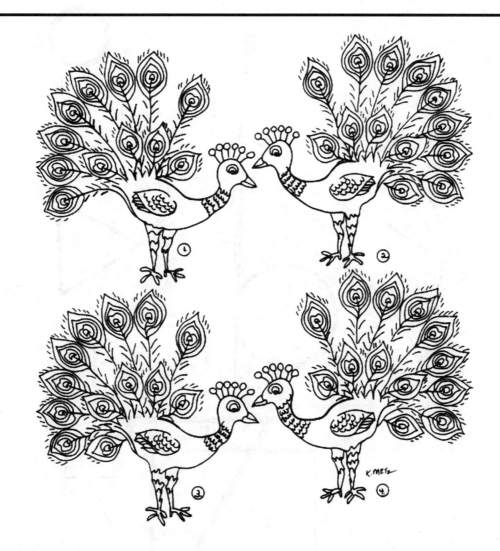

Figure 19.2. Which Peacocks Are Exactly Alike?

Discriminatory Skills

You will need colored pencils or crayons for this exercise.

Use figure 19.3 to do the following:

1.   Outline the largest circle in blue.

2.   Outline the smallest circle in brown.

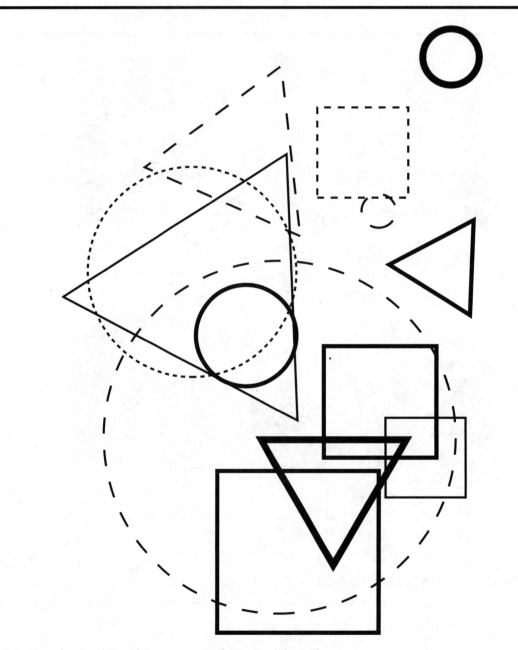

Figure 19.3. Developing Visual Accuracy and Recognizing Closures

3.   Outline all other circles in purple.

4.   Outline the squares in black.

5.   Outline the largest triangle in red.

6.   Outline the smallest triangle in green.

7.   Outline the other triangles in orange.

Perception of Form

Use figure 19.4 to answer the following question.

Which cube matches the original flat pattern?

_____

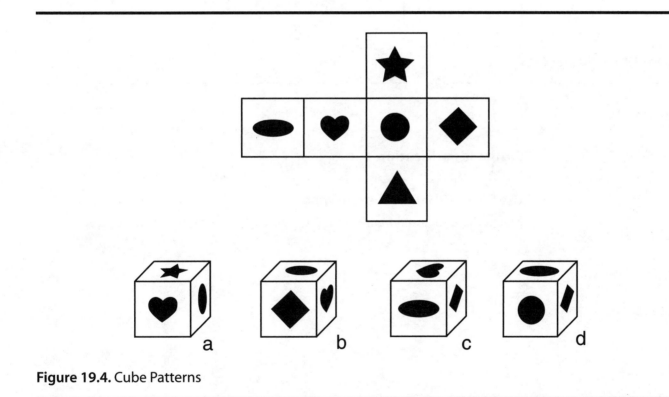

Figure 19.4. Cube Patterns

Use figure 19.5 to answer the following question.

Which of the shapes will fold into an open-end box?

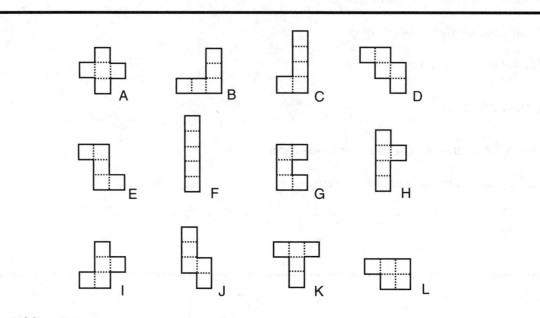

Figure 19.5. Folding Boxes

Figure Identification

Use figure 19.6 to do the following:

Match the individual figures in the top row with the figures in the squares below.

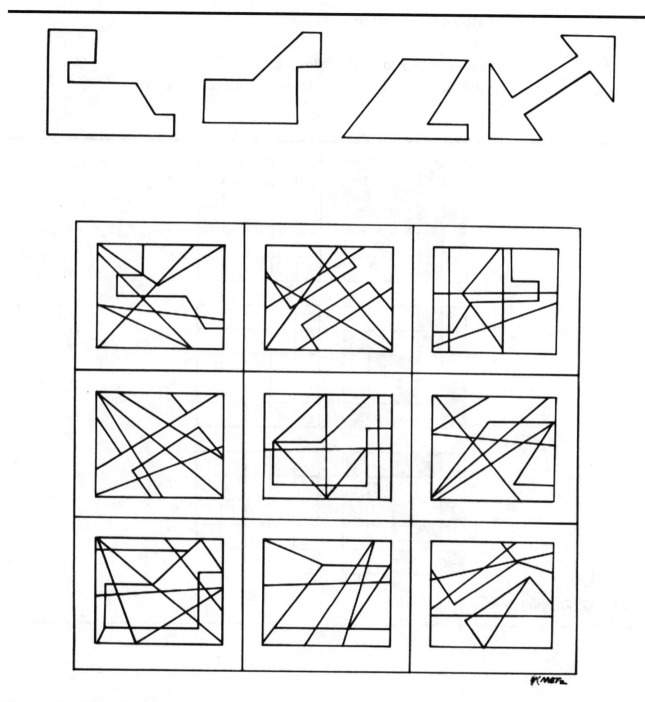

Figure 19.6. Matching Figures

Pattern Duplication

Use figure 19.7 to do the following:
Make the blank grid on the right look like the one on the left.

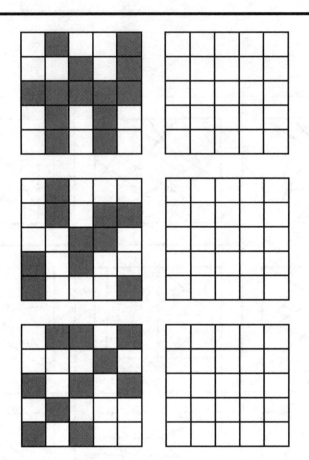

Figure 19.7. Copying Grids

Visualizing Objects in Space

People who create or interpret design prints, including those who build a product, need to be able to visualize objects from several viewpoints.

Use figure 19.8 to do the following:

Look at the diagram of the finished cut card. How can you create that shape from a plain 3"x 5" card? Try it on a plain piece of paper.

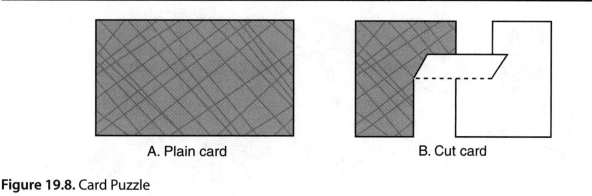

A. Plain card   B. Cut card

Figure 19.8. Card Puzzle

Use figure 19.9 to do the following:

Look at the patterns on the squares. Visualize how you could fold each square so that one punched hole would create the pattern on the square. (If you make a mistake, just try again.)

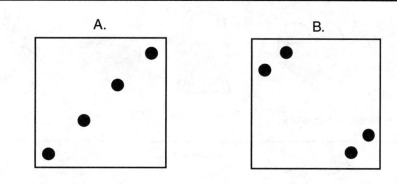

A.   B.

Figure 19.9. Fold and Punch Puzzle

Visual Recall

Use figure 19.10 to do the following:

Look at the pictures for about two minutes, naming all of the items. Now cover the picture and write the names of the pictures you can remember in the spaces provided.

Figure 19.10. How Is Your Visual Memory?

1. _____

2. _____

3. _____

4. _____

5. _____

6. _____

7. _____

8. _____

9. _____

10. _____

11. _____

12. _____

13. _____

14. _____

15. _____

16. _____

17. _____

18. _____

19. _____

20. _____

21. _____

22. _____

23. _____

24. _____

25. _____

How did you do? You can increase your visual memory by doing this exercise once in a while.

Increasing your spatial/visual intelligence is about learning to see and learning to remember objects and details. It may be harder for one person than it is for another, but *everyone* can increase this ability. The payoff for you will be huge. With a little effort, you will increase your ability to see things you have never noticed before. You will increase your visual literacy.

Answer Key

Chapter 1

Check Your Understanding
1. (b) pie chart
2. (c) line graph
3. (b) organization chart
4. (c) bar chart
5. (c) map
6. (a) spreadsheet
7. (c) flowchart
8. (b) problem solving

Your Turn
1. Gantt chart
2. pie chart

Chapter 2

Check Your Understanding
1. Sales Per Associate for Week 12/1-4
2. Sales
3. (b) $200
4. (b) days of the week
5. (c) cloud with rain falling at bottom
6. (c) three parallel lines
7. (a) three triangles of increasing size

8.   (a) strings of different shapes

9.   Answers will vary. One possibility: What were the total sales for each associate?

Chapter 3

Figure 3.5

1.   B3

2.   E2

Figure 3.6

1.   Firestation B

Figure 3.8

1.   approximately 21 miles

Figure 3.9

1.   2000′–2500′

2.   1000′–1500′ higher

Your Turn

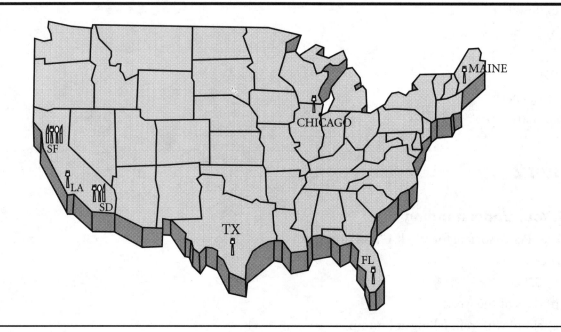

Chapter 4

Figure 4.2

1. (c) $10–$50
2. (c) Saturday
3. (a) Thursday
4. (c) over $100

Figure 4.4

1. 42,200
2. 1,500
3. Charlie

Figure 4.5

1. bathroom cabinet
2. James W.
3. 7
4. It's easy to see where the defects are.

Figure 4.6

1. (b) San Francisco
2. (a) day
3. (c) six
4. (b) #3 (Atlanta, GA)
5. 82 minutes
6. $6.60

Your Turn

Table Usage	Monday People/Tables	Tuesday People/Tables	Wednesday People/Tables	Thursday People/Tables	Total People/Tables
Reading/ Working/ Dirty dishes		1/1	2/2	4/4	7/7
Food customer	3/2	6/3	1/1		10/4
Studying/ no food	16/8	14/7	14/8	7/7	51/30
Empty tables	/1				/1

Chapter 5

Figure 5.2

1. $3,375.20
2. $419.89
3. $3538.48
4. $601.52
5. loan #2
6. loan #2 – 12%
7. $181.63

Figure 5.3

1. (b) February
2. no
3. (b) March
4. (c) increased business income

Figure 5.4

1. $1,000
2. January 2
3. Yes, Jan. 13
4. $1,110.06
5. Yes

Your Turn, Figure 5.5

Balance Column
1,101.66
976.66
892.50
835.72
770.72
584.59
1,484.59
1,384.59

Chapter 6

Figure 6.2
1. Shows number of participants in each age group of each sport.
2. Compares number enrolled in each sport.
3. 6.2a shows the total number in each sport and 6.2b shows individual age groups in each sport.
4. (c) football
5. (b) ice hockey
6. (a) soccer

Figure 6.3
1. (a) They compare the daily sales of each sales associate for each day.
2. (b) Thomas
3. (c) Marie
4. (d) Kate

Figure 6.4
1. (a) It compares the U.S. and California hourly wage median of six occupations.
2. (b) Production Manager
3. (b) Physical Trainers
4. (c) Information not given.

Your Turn

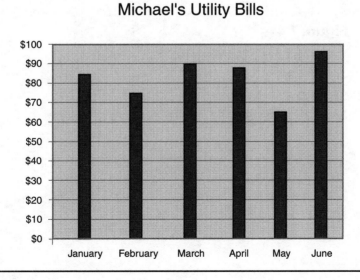

1. Increasing. Although his bills go down in February and May, there is a steady trend upward.
2. June
3. May

Chapter 7

Figure 7.1
1. 50 points
2. December
3. January
4. higher

Figure 7.2
1. (c) Maggie
2. (a) Sol
3. (b) Jeff
4. (c) Maggie
5. (c) Wednesday

Figure 7.3
1. (a) 70 mins.
2. (a) Fri., Sat., Sun.
3. (b) Tues., Thurs., Mon.
4. 60 minutes more
5. 40 minutes

Figure 7.4
1. (b) 3
2. (a) 8
3. (b) 6
4. (b) 16, 20, 24

Your Turn

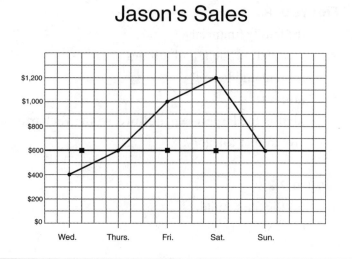

Jason's Sales

---

1. yes
2. above
3. Saturday

Chapter 8

Figure 8.3
1. (c) they are equal
2. (c) 71–90%

Figure 8.5
1. (a) 0–20 minutes
2. yes, nearly so

Figure 8.7
1. (a) yes
2. (b) decrease the time in the 12–17 group

Your Turn
1. B—saw-toothed
2. A—normal distribution
3. D—cliff-like
4. C—bi-modal

Chapter 9

Figure 9.1
1.   (b) family financial
2.   (c) entertainment and utilities
3.   (a) rent and food
4.   (a) rent
      Rent is the largest expenditure, so the Richardsons have the most room to save in that category.

Figure 9.2
1.   (a) Big Shot Builders
2.   (c) GonTuMrow

Figure 9.3
1.   (b) lowest hours
2.   (c) FixIt Quik Inc.
3.   (c) 48 hours
4.   (c) B&C Builders
5.   (a) FixIt Quik
6.   (c) GonTuMrow

Your Turn
1. $76.05; $60.00; $16.05
2.   a. lunch—$22.00

      b. entertainment—$13.00

      c. breakfast—$11.00

      d. clothing—$10.00

      e. personal care—$8.00

      f. transportation—$7.00

      g. school supplies—$6.00

3.

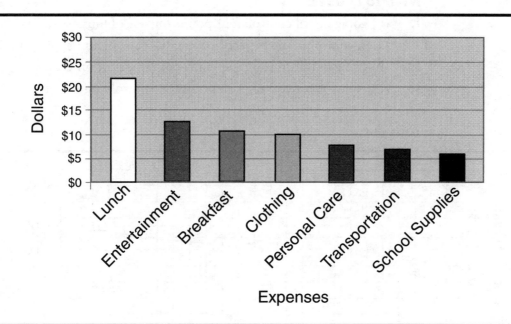

1. food—lunch and breakfast
2. She could keep track of her expenses each day in her log.

Chapter 10

Figure 10.1
1. (b) batch 12
2. (c) batch 1
3. (a) 4 dozen plus

Figure 10.2
1. (a) 8:00 a.m. and 1:00 p.m.
2. (b) 11:00 a.m. and 2:00 p.m.
3. (b) no

Figure 10.5
1. (b) no
2. 3:00 p.m. and 4:00 p.m.

What to Look For

1.   (b) going out of control; four points outside of limits.
2.   (a) in control; all points are between the control limits.
3.   (b) going out of control; too many points near or on UCL.
4.   (b) going out of control; two points on control limits.

Your Turn

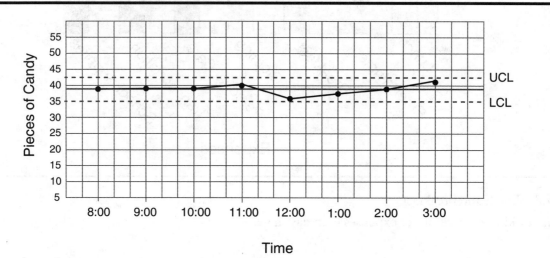

Chapter 11

Figure 11.2

1.   (c) Carl
2.   (b) 3

Figure 11.3

1.   (a) Los Angeles
2.   (d) San Francisco
3.   (a) Los Angeles
4.   (c) Chicago

Figure 11.4

1.   (b) XYZ Company
2.   (c) Executive Offices and M&M Financial

Figure 11.5

1. (b) rent

2. 16%

3. $100

4. (a) rent, food, car

Figure 11.6

1. (a) under 21

2. (b) 79%

3. (d) a theater complex with restaurants

   44% of population is between 21 and 44. A theater complex with restaurants
   would serve that population as well as the under-21 population.

Your Turn

Number of Children per Household in Cementblock City

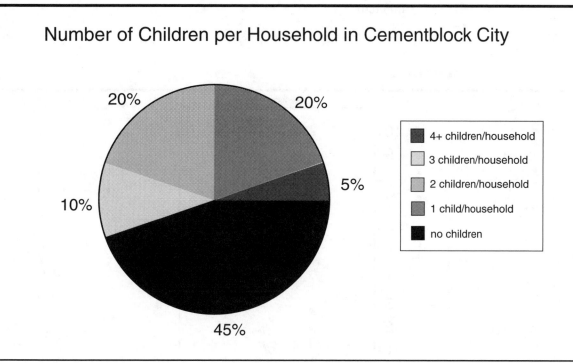

Chapter 12

Figure 12.2

1. 18–30-year-olds

2. 31–50-year-olds

3.   (c) This information is not given. The person who wants to apply this information in this way would probably get information about the theater from someone in the town. Or s/he probably has it. Then s/he could use the age group data to predict whether the theater would meet the needs of the town.

Figure 12.3
1.   misalignment and misplacement
2.   bridges

Figure 12.4
1.   (b) positive
2.   (c) $650/$1000

Figure 12.5
1.   (c) 4:00 p.m.
2.   yes

Your Turn

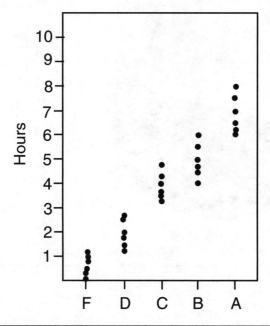

1.   positive
2.   Yes. As the hours of outside reading increase, letter grades go up. There is a positive correlation.

Chapter 13

Figure 13.2

1. methods
2. equipment
3. Answers will vary. A group or individual may have different ideas about which contributing causes need to be investigated further. Further investigation should be objective and factual without the bias of the data gatherer.

Figure 13.3

1. people
2. people

Figure 13.4

1. methods
2. methods
3. Answers will vary. A group or individual may have different ideas about where causes belong on a fishbone diagram.

Your Turn

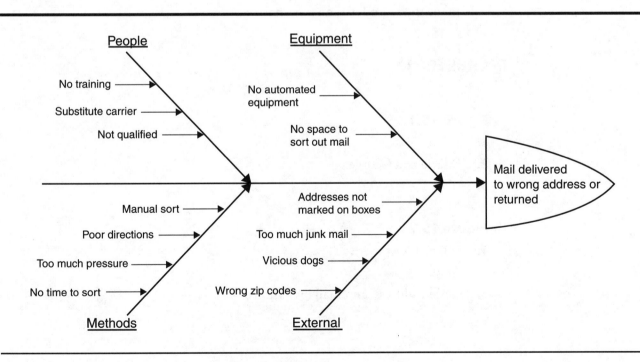

Chapter 14

Figure 14.2

1. Using your new computer
2. buy a computer
3. learn the keyboard
4. next challenge
5. Any of the following: training, self-instruction, process clarification and improvement, documenting processes

Figure 14.3

1. How to Host a Party
2. 13
3. 14
4. Answers will vary.
5. Answers will vary.

Your Turn

Answers will vary. One way to check yourself is to show it to someone and go through the steps with him/her. Encourage him/her to ask questions. You will be able to see if you understand flowcharting.

Chapter 15

Figure 15.1

1. John
2. Marie and George
3. five

Figure 15.2

1. August–October
2. July
3. order, address, and mail invitations

Figure 15.3

1. the team
2. May
3. No
4. design phases 1, 2, 3

Figure 15.4

1. March 31
2. certify two in-house trainers
3. February

Figure 15.5

1. 30 days
2. 2 weeks

Your Turn

Soccer Season Gantt Chart										
Action/Activity	March	April	May	June	July	Aug	Sept	Oct	Nov	Dec
Hold try outs		▓								
Select team		▓								
Hold parent meeting		▓								
Set up meeting			▓							
Practice			▓	▓	▓	▓				
Enter tournaments			▓							
Order uniforms			▓							
Play games				▓	▓	▓	▓			

Chapter 16

Figure 16.2

1. Great-Grandma and Great-Grandpa Mattel, Great-Grandma and Great-Grandpa Plastic
2. Twinkle Toes and Hollywood Star

Figure 16.3

1. (a) Northern
2. (b) 4
3. (b) it is a good way to get information from all areas

Figure 16.4

1. 3/23 at 8:00 a.m.
2. 3/24 at 2:00 p.m.

Figure 16.5

1. borrow money
2. earn money

Figure 16.7

1. Director of Operations
2. Great Leader and Chief Executive Officer of Great Company
3. Director of Quality Assurance
4. Supervisor of Unimportant Large Products

Your Turn

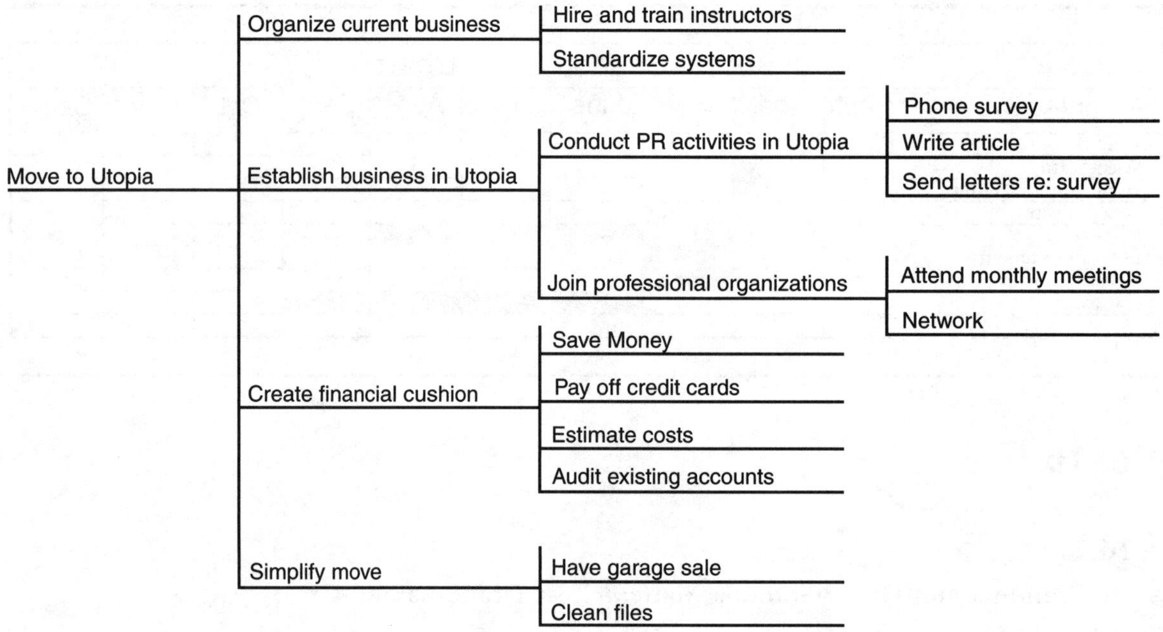

Move to Utopia	Organize current business	Hire and train instructors	
		Standardize systems	
	Establish business in Utopia	Conduct PR activities in Utopia	Phone survey
			Write article
			Send letters re: survey
		Join professional organizations	Attend monthly meetings
			Network
	Create financial cushion	Save Money	
		Pay off credit cards	
		Estimate costs	
		Audit existing accounts	
	Simplify move	Have garage sale	
		Clean files	

Chapter 17

Figure 17.2
1.   Bracket
2.   865340-2
3.   1 of 2
4.   2
5.   J. Smith
6.   9-4-99
7.   SA 1280 Steel
8.   HDN to Rc58

Your Turn
Answers will vary. Check your drawing by reviewing the chapter and referring to it as you check.

Chapter 18

Check Your Understanding
1.   (b) symbols
2.   (c) location of parts of the building's electrical system
3.   (a) block diagram
4.   (a) the operation of a circuit from beginning to end

Your Turn

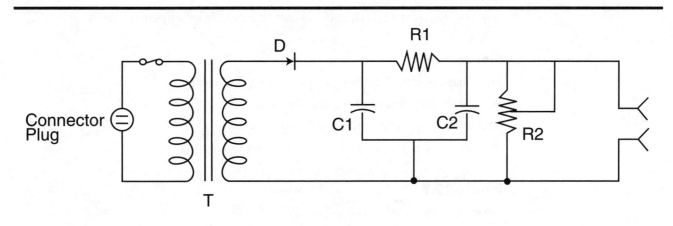

Chapter 19

Figure 19.1

1. Two.
2. You should be able to see both an old woman and a young woman. If you can't, here is a hint: the cheekbone and chin of the young woman become the nose of the old woman.
3. When you find a high step, it turns into the low step of the next staircase. Actually, the model is two staircases separated at the right stair.
4. Same as #3
5. Each pair of lines is a cylinder at one end and a rectangle at the other. You have to carefully draw what is there, not what you see when you first look at it.

Figure 19.2

1. 2 and 3
2. Count the rings on the necks, count the number of feathers in each row of the tail, and look closely at the patterns on the legs.

Figure 19.3

Check the directions and the colors of your shapes to make sure you followed directions.

Figure 19.4

(a)

Figure 19.5

(A), (C), (E), (H), (I), (J), and (K) can all be made into open-end boxes.

Figure 19.6

First shape is found in the square in the top left corner.
Second shape is found in the middle square.
Third shape is found in the right middle square.
Fourth shape is found in the bottom right corner square.

Figure 19.7

No answer required

Figure 19.8

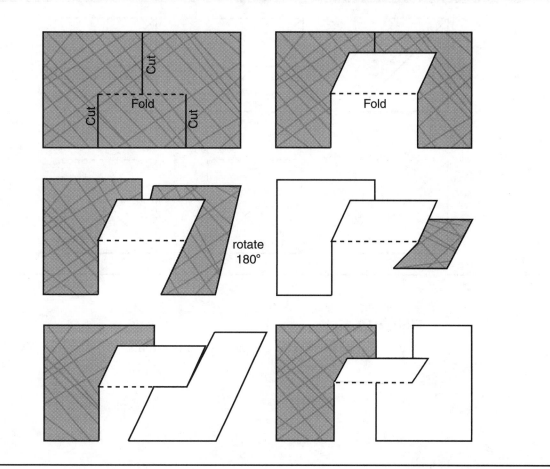

Figure 19.9

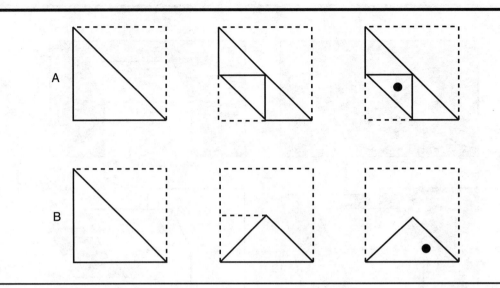

Figure 19.10

Check your answers with the pictures of the items.

Posttest

Now that you've spent a good deal of time improving your ability to process information presented visually, take this posttest to see how much you've learned. If you took the pretest at the beginning of this book, you have a good way to compare what you knew when you started the book with what you know now.

When you complete this test, grade yourself, and then compare your score with your score on the pretest. If your score now is much greater than your pretest score, congratulations—you've profited noticeably from your hard work. If your score shows little improvement, perhaps there are certain chapters you need to review. Do you notice a pattern to the types of questions you got wrong? Whatever you score on this posttest, keep this book around for review and to refer to when you are unsure of how to read a visual graphic.

Take as much time as you need to do this short test. Simply circle the answers in the book. If this book does not belong to you, write the numbers 1–35 on a piece of paper and record your answers there. When you finish, check your answers against the answer key that follows this test. Each answer tells you which lesson of this book teaches you about the type of chart or graph in that question.

Use the map on the next page to answer questions 1–3.

1. Candi Barr has a day job at General Hospital and performs a theatrical act at night at the Star Theatre. She must go home between jobs to change from her surgical scrubs to her theatrical costume. Which of the following bus lines will get her from the hospital to her home at Johnson and Elm to the Star Theatre most directly?

   a. 37 and 42   b. 21 and 37   c. 37 and 17

2. Bob Hinkel is a guard at the penitentiary and takes a night course in botany at State University. Which bus route(s) will get him from his job to his class most quickly and directly?

   a. 59 and walk east   b. 33 and walk west   c. 21 and walk west

3. After a pleasant afternoon feeding the squirrels in North Park, Ruth decides to spend an hour at the Ocean Museum before heading home. Which bus route(s) will get her there most quickly and directly?

   a. 37 and 21   b. 37 and 59   c. 17 and 37

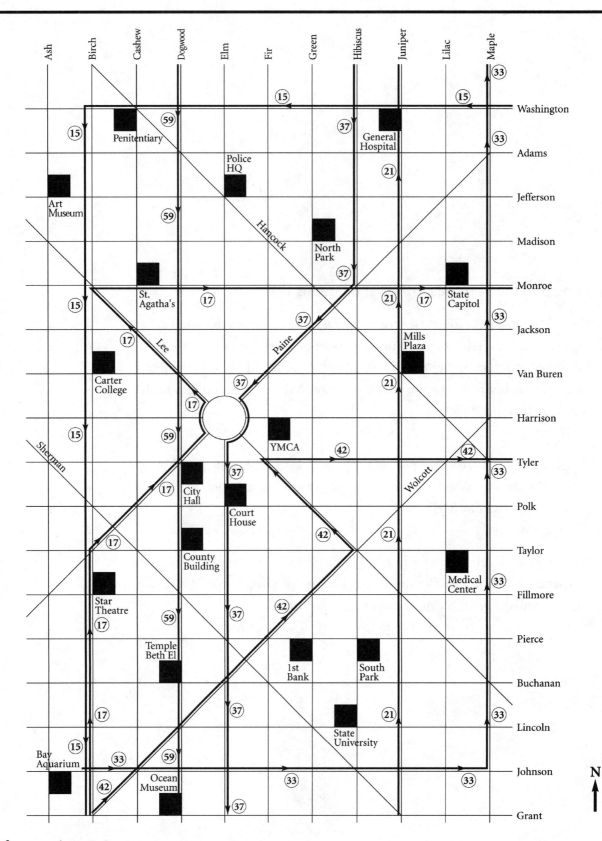

Map for questions 1–3

Route # 72 Schedule

Lv Elm & Oak Sts	Arr Linn & Maple Sts	Arr Pine & Ash Sts	Arr Willow & Apple Sts	Arr Pear & Beech Sts	Arr Fir & Linder Sts
6:30 AM	6:35 AM	6:42 AM	6:44 AM	6:50 AM	6:52 AM
7:00	7:05	7:12	7:14	7:20	7:22
7:30	7:35	7:42	7:44	7:50	7:52
8:00	8:05	8:12	8:14	8:20	8:22
8:30	8:35	8:42	8:44	8:50	8:52

Bus schedule for question 4

Use the bus schedule to answer question 4.

4. A passenger boards the bus at Pine & Ash Streets at 7:42. What time will the passenger arrive at Pear & Beech Streets?

   a. 7:20   b. 7:50   c. 8:20

EFFICIENCY LOG

for Monday July 12

ACTIVITY	8:00–10:00	10:00–12:00	1:00–3:00	3:00–5:00
Personal phone calls	xxxx xx	xxxx	xxxx x	xxxx xxx
Incidents of chatting, unrelated to work	xxxx xxx	xxxx xx	xxxx xxx	xxxx xx
Unauthorized vending machine breaks	xxxx xx	xxxx x	xxx	xxxx xxxx

Efficiency log for questions 5 and 6

Use the efficiency log to answer questions 5 and 6.

5. Dudmire Insurance Co. has hired an efficiency expert, who is keeping a log of time-wasting infractions engaged in by employees. The expert makes a small "x" whenever an instance of time-wasting occurs. At what time of day do most infractions occur?

   a. 8:00–10:00

   b. 10:00–12:00

   c. 1:00–3:00

   d. 3:00–5:00

6. On which type of activity will the Dudmire management have to crack down hardest?

    a. personal phone calls   b. chatting   c. unauthorized breaks

Date	Minimum Payment due	Payment Made	Balance $200	Interest 22%	New Balance
1/3/99	$40	$40	$160.00	$35.20	$195.20
2/3/99	$40	$40	$155.20	$34.14	$189.34
3/3/99	$40	$40	$149.34	$32.85	$182.19
4/3/99	$40	$10			

Table for question 7

Use the table to answer question 7.

7. Just before its manager is indicted for fraud and racketeering, the Quik n' Easy Loan Company makes a loan of $200 to Luella Perkins so she can buy a birthday gift for her grandson. As shown on the spreadsheet, 22% interest is to be added to the unpaid balance at the end of each month. What will happen if Luella can pay only $10 in April?

    a. She will owe more than her original loan amount.

    b. She will owe the same as her original loan amount.

    c. She will owe less than her original loan amount.

Use the graph on the next page to answer questions 8 and 9.

8. The graph has been developed to aid state police personnel responsible for patrolling a certain stretch of interstate highway. The most likely immediate purpose of the graph is to help with decisions about

    a. programs needed to better the relationship between state police and paramedics

    b. the number of state police personnel needed on particular shifts

    c. adding a second driving course to the ones that already exist in the nearest town

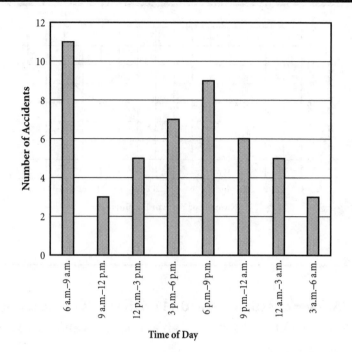

Graph for questions 8 and 9

9. Which of the following is true for the period during the hours of 3 p.m. and 6 p.m.?

a. More accidents occur than between 3 a.m. and 6 a.m., but fewer than between 6 a.m. and 9 a.m.

b. Fewer accidents occur than between 6 p.m. and 9 p.m. but more than between 6 a.m. and 9 a.m.

c. Fewer accidents occur than between 6 a.m. and 9. a.m. and between 12 a.m. and 3 a.m.

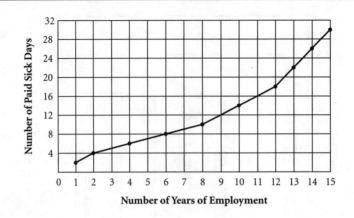

Graph for questions 10 and 11.

Answer questions 10 and 11 on the basis of the graph, which shows the number of paid sick days an employee is allowed over 15 years of employment.

10. What is the most logical purpose for this graph?
    a. a cautionary note to employees not to call in sick too often
    b. part of an explanation of benefits for new employees
    c. proof that older employees call in sick more often
    d. an insert into the packet of information given retirees

11. About how many more paid sick days can an employee take after 11 years than after 6 years?
    a. 5   b. 6   c. 7   d. 8

Frequency Table of Number of Personal Phone Calls

Employee	Frequency	Total
Mariah	xx	2
Bob	xxxx	4
Jeeter	xxxxxxxxxxxx	12
Tanya	xxxxxxxxx	7
Pete	x	1

Frequency table for question 12

Use the frequency table to answer question 12.

12. The proprietor of Bubba's Barbecue has been receiving complaints about slow service and has decided it is because the members of his waitstaff spend too much time on the phone. He has decided to use a frequency curve to decide whom to fire.

   Based on the frequency curve, which two employees should Bubba fire?
   a. Bob and Jeeter   b. Jeeter and Tanya   c. Mariah and Pete

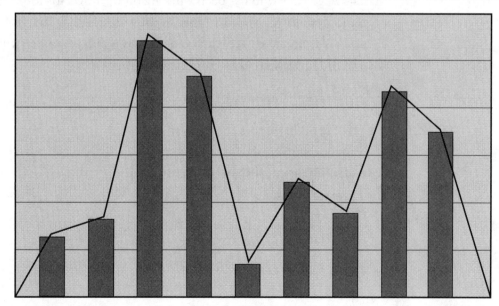

Histogram for question 13

Use the histogram to answer question 13.

13. The histogram shown is a good example of a
   a. cliff-like curve   b. skewed curve   c. saw-toothed curve

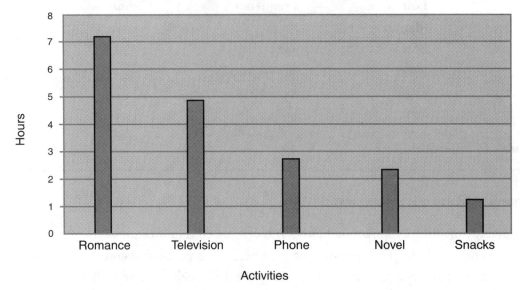

Pareto chart for questions 14 and 15

Use the chart to answer questions 14 and 15.

14. Marcus is a writer who has been working on his novel for four years, and has begun to despair of ever finishing. In order to identify the problem, he has created a Pareto chart. Which two activities will have to be switched, time-wise, in order for Marcus to come nearer his goal?

   _____

15. What is the main purpose of a Pareto chart?
   a. to analyze statistical data
   b. to identify the most significant issue
   c. to prove a point

16. Following are lines that might be found on a control chart.

Suppose points are laid along these lines to make a line graph. Now suppose several of these points lie outside the upper control line. Considering the general purpose of a control chart, this should alert the chart user that the process being charted is

a. going better than expected

b. going out of control

c. impossible to tell from the information given

17. The main purpose of a run chart is to

a. solve a mathematical problem

b. compare sets of data from two separate sources

c. show a trend

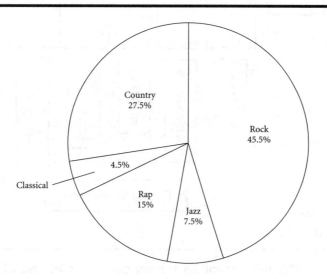

Pie chart for questions 18 and 19

Use the pie chart to answer questions 18 and 19.

18. A popular music store, Music-O-Rama, sells compact discs in the distribution shown on the pie chart. Which type of music is twice as popular as which other type?

a. Rock is twice as popular as country.

b. Country is twice as popular as rap.

c. Rap is twice as popular as jazz.

19. On the basis of compact disc sales, which of the following concerts would likely draw the biggest audience in this town?
    a. Tex Wilson and his Good Ole Boys Live!
    b. Blue Hill Quartet for Strings & Oboe
    c. Dixieland Saturday Night at the Blue Fox Club

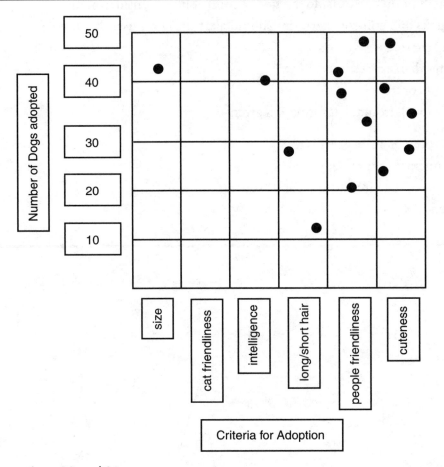

Number of Dogs adopted

50

40

30

20

10

size | cat friendliness | intelligence | long/short hair | people friendliness | cuteness

Criteria for Adoption

Point graph for questions 20 and 21

Use the point graph to answer questions 20 and 21.

20. Which two criteria were most important to would-be dog owners?

_____

Explain your answer.

_____

21. It can be deduced from the graph that most of the people adopting a dog
    a. did not care what kind of dog they got, as long as it was healthy
    b. wanted the adopted dog to serve as a watchdog
    c. either did not own a cat or did not like their cat

22. The fishbone diagram also goes by another name, which describes its function. That name is
    a. the cause-and-effect diagram
    b. the correlative diagram
    c. the efficiency diagram

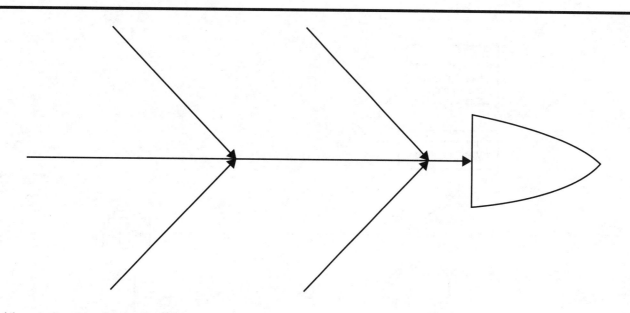

Fishbone diagram for question 23

Use the fishbone diagram to answer question 23.

23. Write on the diagram where the problem or effect would go and where the possible causes would go.

Use the flowchart on the next page to answer questions 24 and 25.

24. How can you tell that "Get a dog" is not really meant to be a step in the process?

_____

25. What do the diamonds on the flowchart represent?
    a. decision points in a process
    b. the beginning or end of a process
    c. steps in a process

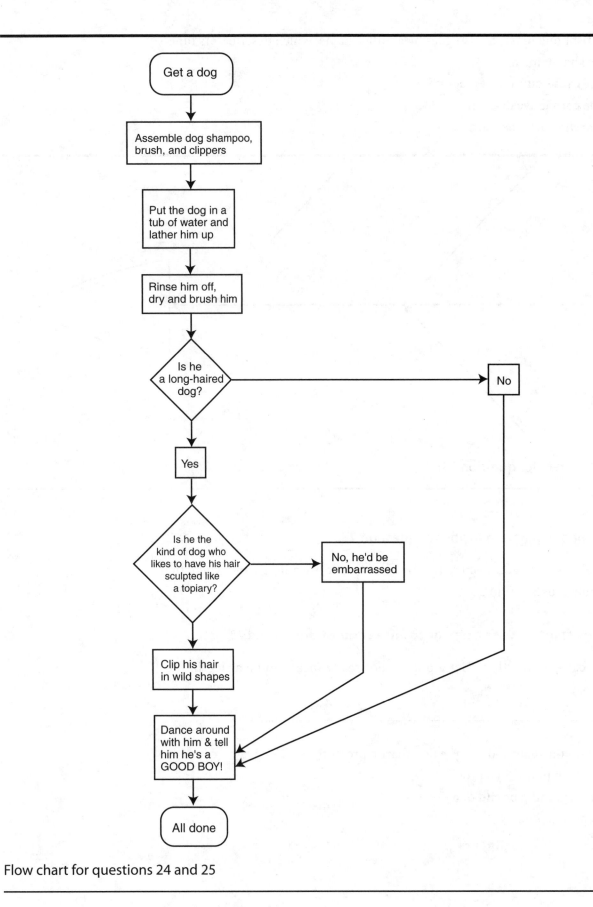

Flow chart for questions 24 and 25

Tim's Cleaning Schedule

	Sun.	Mon.	Tues.	Wed.	Thurs.	Fri.	Sat.	Sun.
Clean bedroom closet	▓							
Clean kitchen		▓						
Clean living room			▓					
Wash dog				▓				
Clean bathroom					▓	▓		
Do laundry							▓	
Shop for food								▓

Gantt chart for questions 26 and 27

Use the Gantt chart to answer questions 26 and 27.

26. It is Sunday, and Tim is expecting his parents to arrive one week from Monday. His apartment is a mess, so he decides to create a scheduling Gantt chart to make sure everything gets done. According to the chart, which room in Tim's apartment is probably the most disgusting?
    a. the bedroom closet
    b. the kitchen
    c. the living room
    d. the bathroom

27. If Tim's parents arrive a day early, at 5:00 a.m., what will they most likely find?
    a. a muddy dog
    b. an unsightly bathroom
    c. piles of dirty clothes everywhere
    d. insufficient food for supper

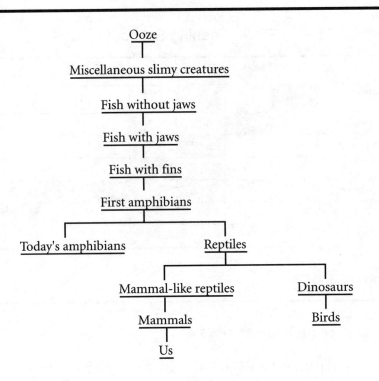

Tree diagram for question 28 and 29

Use the tree diagram to answer questions 28 and 29.

28. The diagram is a kind of evolutionary family tree, starting with slime and ending with human beings, and is called a "divergent" tree graph. The name comes from the fact that
    a. each branch represents an autonomous entity
    b. the origin of the branches is the most significant entry
    c. all branches fork from a single branch

29. On the diagram, from what group did the mammal-like reptiles most directly descend?
    a. first amphibians
    b. dinosaurs
    c. reptiles

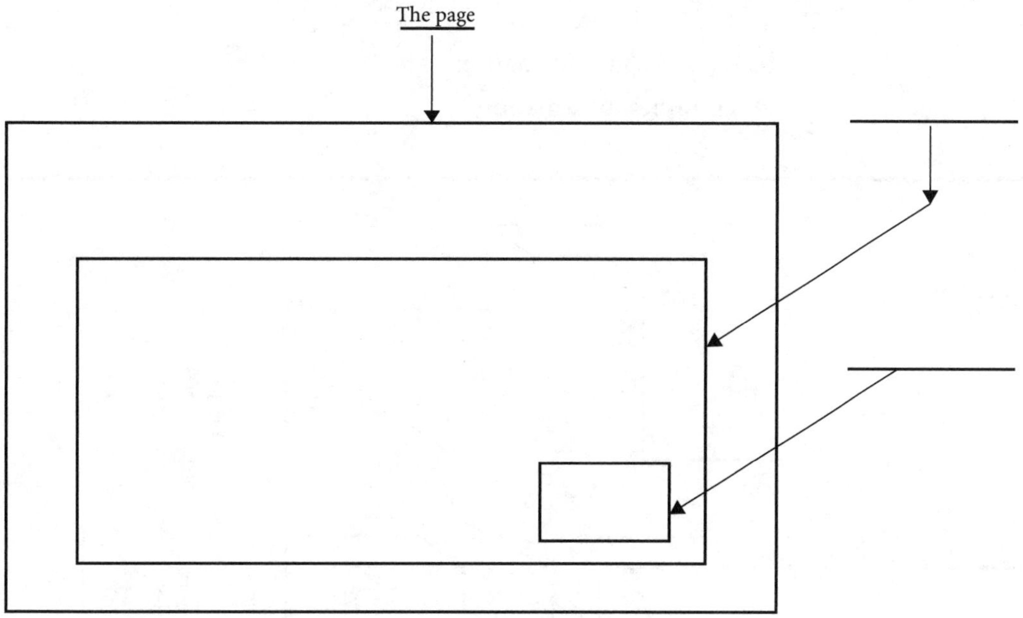

Blueprint diagram for question 30.

Use the blueprint diagram to answer question 30.

30. Label the parts of the blueprint.

Use the electronics diagram to answer question 31.

31. What do symbols A and B in the graphic stand for?

a. A = buzzer; B = amplifier

b. A = fuse, n-p-n; B = microphone

c. A = transformer; B = ground, general

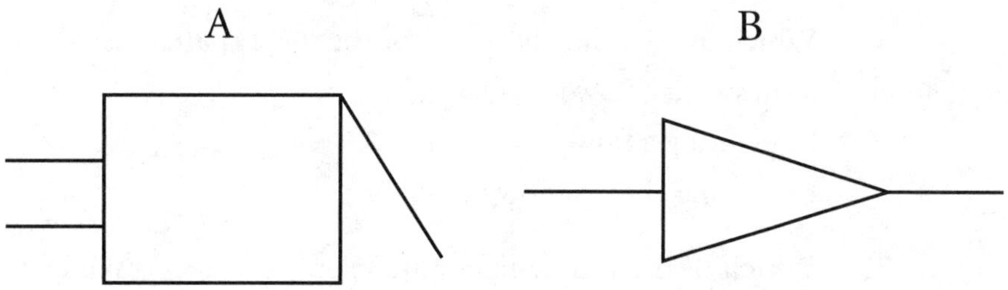

Electronics diagram for question 31

32. What does a block diagram do?

 a. itemizes information

 b. expands on information

 c. simplifies information

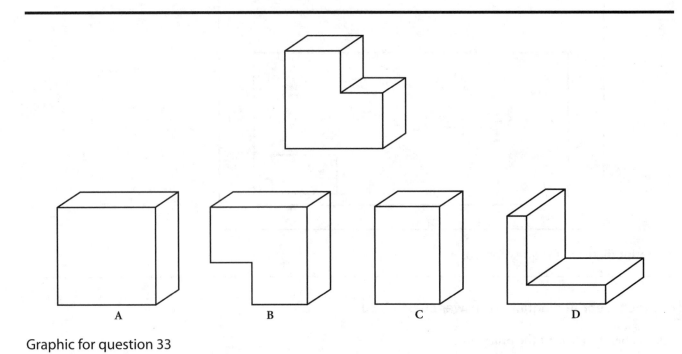

Graphic for question 33

Use the graphic to answer question 33.

33. Which of the four lettered figures could be the unlettered (top) figure, seen from a different angle?

 a. B only   b. A and B   c. B and C   d. B and D

34. Which of the following calls for the most spatial/visual intelligence?

 a. drawing a flower

 b. planting a flower

 c. reading about a flower

35. Which of the following would exercise your visual/spatial intelligence the LEAST?

 a. looking at optical illusions

 b. making origami (Japanese paper flowers)

 c. playing the flute

Answers

1.   **c.** 37 from the hospital to home, then the 17 (after a short walk) to the theatre.

2.   **a.** Bob should take the 59 and walk 4 blocks east.

3.   **b.** The 37 is closest to both ends of the route, but the 59 will also work.

4.   **b.** Read the "Pine & Ash" column down to the third row, where you find 7:42; then read across to the "Pear & Beech" column.

5.   **d.** Most infractions are in the 3:00–5:00 time period.

6.   **b.** There are 26 instances of chatting.

7.   **a.** Interest in March was $32.85. It will be a little less in April, if Luella pays $10—but not much. It would take a difference between payment ($10) and interest ($30+) of less than $20 to bring the new balance over $200.

8.   **b.** The fact that the horizontal axis on the graph deals with time of day makes choice **b** most logical. Time of day would not specifically relate to the other two choices.

9.   **a.** Compare the lengths of the three bars.

10. **b.** The graph deals with the sick leave benefits of employees and is not concerned with how often an employee calls in sick. Choice **d** is wrong because a retiree would not have use for information about sick leave.

11. **d.** After 11 years, an employee gets 16 sick days; after 6, 8 sick days.

12. **b.** Jeeter and Tanya made the most calls followed (distantly) by Bob. Bubba should definitely hang onto Mariah and Pete, who made the fewest calls!

13. **c.** The name is descriptive of the shape of the curve. This curve shows no pattern of development; the distribution is random.

14. Unfortunately, Marcus will have to spend less time on his love life, switching romance and novel.

15. **b.** In Marcus's case, the purpose is to identify exactly where he is being unproductive in pursuing his goal of finishing his novel.

16. **b.** The purpose of a control chart, as the name indicates, is to make sure a process remains within certain limits—for example, that batches of a cookie dough mix yield the same number of cookies (see chapter 10). Any time points stray outside the upper and lower control lines, the process is going out of control.

17. **c.** A run chart shows a record of data over a sequential period of time and so can be used to identify a trend.

18. **c.** 7.5 % × 2 =15%.

19. **a.** Country would definitely be the winner in this town.

20. People-friendliness and cuteness were the most important criteria. The greatest number of points on the graph are concentrated in these two cells.

21. **c.** No one adopted a dog on with an eye to cat-friendliness.
22. **a.** Fishbone diagrams are also known as cause-and-effect diagrams.
23. On the fishbone diagram, the problem or effect is written on the "head" of the fish and the possible causes on the parts of its "skeleton."
24. Because the phrase is in an oval, rather than in a rectangle.
25. **a.** Diamonds represent decision points.
26. **d.** Tim has set aside two days to clean the bathroom.
27. **d.** Tim is planning to shop for food on Sunday, but it's doubtful he'll have done so by 5:00 a.m.
28. **c.** All branches fork or *diverge* from a single branch.
29. **c.** To find the answer, start at "mammal-like reptiles" and follow the only line that goes up one level.
30. The larger rectangle on the page is the Print Body. The smaller rectangle on the page is the Title Block.
31. **a.** The part labeled A is the buzzer; B is the amplifier.
32. **c.** A block diagram can be used to simplify information.
33. **a.** Figure B is the unlettered object rotated 180°.
34. **a.** Drawing calls for the greatest ability to visualize details of an object in space.
35. **c.** Playing the flute would test your musical intelligence, but would not require that you visualize objects in space.

Bibliography

Allen, James P., and Eugene Turner, *The Ethnic Quilt*. Northridge: The Center for Geographical Studies, California State University, 1997.

Brassard, Michael, and Diane Ritter, *The Memory Jogger*. Meuthen, MA: Goal/QPC, 1994.

Burban, Peter, Marshall L. Schmitt, and Charles G. Carter, Jr., *Understanding Electricity and Electronics Technology*. New York: McGraw Hill, 1987.

Clarke, Brynly, *The Way Excel for Macintosh Works*. Bothwell, WA: Microsoft Press, 1994.

Cowley, Michael, and Ellen Domb, *Beyond Strategic Vision*. Boston: Butterworth-Heinemann, 1997.

Garner, Howard, *Frames of Mind*. New York: Basic Books, 1993.

Harris, Robert L., *Information Graphics: A Comprehensive Illustrated Reference*. Atlanta: Management Graphics, 1996.

Hoffman, Edward G., and Paul R. Wallach, *Blueprint Reading for Manufacturing*. Albany: Delmar, 1988.

Juran, J.M., *Juran on Quality by Design*. New York: Free Press, 1992.

Kelly, Michael R., *Everyone's Problem-Solving Handbook*. New York: Quality Resources, 1992.

Miller, Mark, and Rex Miller, *Electronics The Easy Way*. Hauppauge, NY: Barron's, 1995.

Richey, David, *Team Problem Solving Process*. Ventura, CA: Quality Groups Publishing, 1991.

Tufte, Edward R., *Envisioning Information*. Cheshire, CN: Graphics Press, 1990.

Tufte, Edward R., *The Visual Display of Information*. Cheshire, CN: Graphics Press, 1983.

Whitely, Richard C., *The Customer Driven Company*. Reading, MA: Addison Wesley, 1991.